The Rise of Artificial Intelligence Impact on Industries and Society

The Rise of Artificial Intelligence Impact on Industries and Society

Rayan Musk

UNIEK ENTERPRISES

CONTENTS

Table of Content

Chapter 1

Foundations of Artificial Intelligence

Groundworks of Man-made consciousness (computer based intelligence) include a range of standards, strategies, and techniques that support the turn of events and working of insightful frameworks. As we dig into the basic components of man-made intelligence, it becomes evident that this interdisciplinary field draws motivation from different parts of science, math, and designing. From AI calculations to brain organizations, the underpinnings of artificial intelligence are well established in the journey to repeat and upgrade human mental capacities in machines.

AI:

At the core of man-made intelligence lies AI, a subfield that enables frameworks to gain and improve as a matter of fact without being expressly modified. AI calculations empower PCs to perceive designs, make expectations, and adjust to evolving conditions. The underpinning of AI is laid upon the accessibility of tremendous datasets, computational power, and modern calculations that can observe complex examples inside the information.

Directed Learning:

Directed learning is a principal worldview inside AI, where a model is prepared on a named dataset. In this methodology, the calculation figures out how to plan contributions to wanted yields, copying the course of an educator giving named guides to an understudy. Normal applications incorporate picture acknowledgment, discourse to-text, and spam sifting.

Unaided Learning:

Conversely, solo learning includes preparing a model on unlabeled information, moving the framework to independently recognize examples and connections. Grouping and dimensionality decrease are predominant solo learning strategies. This essential idea empowers machines to reveal stowed away designs inside information without unequivocal direction.

Support Learning:

Support learning presents the idea of a specialist collaborating with a climate to accomplish an objective. The specialist gets criticism as remunerations or punishments in light of its activities, empowering it to learn ideal methodologies through experimentation. This essential idea is especially pivotal in situations where machines should pursue successive choices, like game-playing and independent frameworks.

Brain Organizations:

Brain networks structure the foundation of numerous computer based intelligence applications, drawing motivation from the many-sided engineering of the human mind. These computational models comprise of interconnected hubs coordinated in layers. Every association between hubs has a weight, and during preparing, these loads are changed in light of info information and wanted yield. The profundity and construction of brain networks lead to the expression "profound learning," a methodology that has shown amazing progress in errands like picture and discourse acknowledgment.

Profound Learning:

Profound learning, a subset of AI, includes brain networks with various layers, frequently alluded to as profound brain organizations. The profundity of these organizations permits them to extricate progressive highlights from information, prompting predominant execution in complex assignments naturally. Convolutional Brain Organizations (CNNs) succeed in picture related errands, while Repetitive Brain Organizations (RNNs) are compelling in dealing with consecutive information.

Information and Huge Information:

The meaning of information couldn't possibly be more significant in that frame of mind of computer based intelligence. The accessibility of huge and different datasets is urgent for preparing AI models actually.

Enormous Information advances, which include the handling and investigation of monstrous datasets, synergize with artificial intelligence to open bits of knowledge and examples that would be illogical to recognize utilizing customary strategies. The exchange among man-made intelligence and Huge Information has pushed headways in different areas, from medical care to fund.

Calculations and Algorithmic Intricacy:

Calculations act as the scholarly motors of computer based intelligence frameworks, organizing the means engaged with tackling a particular issue. The proficiency and viability of these calculations assume a urgent part in the general presentation of simulated intelligence applications. The idea of algorithmic intricacy, or how computational assets scale with the size of the info, turns out to be especially important in advancing man-made intelligence calculations for true applications.

Normal Language Handling (NLP):

Normal Language Handling is an essential idea inside man-made intelligence that spotlights on the cooperation among PCs and human language. NLP empowers machines to comprehend, decipher, and produce human-like text. Applications range from chatbots and language interpretation to feeling investigation and text outline. The groundworks of NLP include etymological standards, factual models, and, all the more as of late, profound learning strategies.

PC Vision:

PC Vision, one more foundation of artificial intelligence, bestows machines with the capacity to decipher and settle on choices in light of visual information. This essential idea tracks down applications in facial acknowledgment, object recognition, and independent vehicles. PC vision calculations frequently influence profound gaining designs to remove significant data from pictures and recordings.

Morals and Predisposition in artificial intelligence:

The moral contemplations implanted in the underpinnings of simulated intelligence are principal. As artificial intelligence frameworks go with choices that influence people and society, inquiries of predisposition, decency, straightforwardness, and responsibility become focal. The moral underpinnings of simulated intelligence include tending to predispositions in preparing information, guaranteeing algorithmic straightforwardness, and laying out systems for dependable simulated intelligence advancement and organization.

Protection and Security:

The underpinnings of computer based intelligence additionally converge with protection and security concerns. As computer based intelligence frameworks process immense measures of individual information, guaranteeing the protection of people turns into a basic thought.

Safety efforts should be executed to defend simulated intelligence models from pernicious assaults, which can have extensive results in delicate areas like medical services and money.

Interdisciplinary Nature of computer based intelligence:

The underpinnings of artificial intelligence are innately interdisciplinary, drawing from software engineering, math, mental science, neuroscience, and different designing disciplines. The mixture of information from these assorted areas adds to the all encompassing comprehension and improvement of astute frameworks.

Future Patterns:

As the underpinnings of computer based intelligence keep on developing, a few future patterns shape the direction of the field. Reasonable computer based intelligence, which centers around making computer based intelligence frameworks more justifiable and interpretable, is acquiring noticeable quality. Combined realizing, where models are prepared across decentralized gadgets to save security, addresses a change in how man-made intelligence calculations work. Quantum registering, with its capability to change calculation, presents energizing opportunities for handling complex computer based intelligence issues.

1.1 Machine Learning and Deep Learning

AI and profound learning are significant parts of man-made reasoning, reshaping the scene of how PCs learn and simply decide. These fields address a change in perspective from conventional rule-based programming, permitting machines to obtain information and further develop execution through experience. As we investigate the subtleties of AI and profound learning, it becomes obvious that they support a bunch of uses, from picture acknowledgment to normal language handling, driving groundbreaking progressions across businesses.

AI:

At its center, AI is a subset of computerized reasoning that spotlights on the improvement of calculations equipped for gaining from information. In contrast to customary programming, where unequivocal guidelines direct the way in which a framework ought to act, AI frameworks gain examples and connections from input information. The essential reason is to empower PCs to sum up from models, pursuing expectations or choices in new, concealed circumstances.

Managed Learning:

Directed learning is a foundation of AI, addressing a worldview where the calculation is prepared on a marked dataset. Named information comprises of info yield matches, where the result addresses the ideal result.

The model figures out how to plan contributions to comparing yields, successfully catching the connection between the elements and the objective variable. Normal utilizations of directed learning incorporate picture acknowledgment, discourse acknowledgment, and spam sifting.

Solo Learning:

Solo learning, conversely, includes preparing a model on unlabeled information, provoking the framework to freely recognize examples and designs. Bunching, where the calculation bunches comparable information focuses together, and dimensionality decrease, which improves on complex datasets while holding fundamental data, are predominant solo learning methods. Solo learning is instrumental in uncovering stowed away designs inside information and extricating significant bits of knowledge without unequivocal direction.

Support Learning:

Support learning presents the idea of a specialist connecting with a climate and learning through experimentation. The specialist gets criticism as remunerations or punishments in view of its activities, permitting it to adjust and refine its procedures after some time. This central idea is especially relevant in situations where a specialist should settle on a succession of choices, like in game-playing or independent frameworks.

Profound Learning:

Profound learning addresses a subfield of AI that use brain networks with various layers, frequently alluded to as profound brain organizations. The profundity of these organizations permits them to naturally learn progressive portrayals of information, separating perplexing highlights at various levels. Profound learning has exhibited surprising progress in undertakings, for example, picture and discourse acknowledgment, normal language handling, and in any event, playing complex games like Go.

Brain Organizations:

Brain networks are computational models enlivened by the engineering and working of the human mind. These organizations comprise of interconnected hubs, or neurons, coordinated in layers. Every association between hubs has a weight, and during preparing, these loads are changed in view of info information and the ideal result. The layers in a brain network incorporate an information layer, at least one secret layers, and a result layer. The method involved with changing loads during preparing empowers brain organizations to learn complex examples and portrayals.

Convolutional Brain Organizations (CNNs):

Convolutional Brain Organizations (CNNs) are a specific kind of brain network intended for handling and examining visual information, like pictures and recordings.

CNNs are outfitted with convolutional layers that apply channels to include information, catching spatial pecking orders of highlights. This design is especially compelling in picture acknowledgment undertakings, where progressive examples and designs assume a vital part.

Repetitive Brain Organizations (RNNs):

Repetitive Brain Organizations (RNNs) are intended to deal with consecutive information, making them appropriate for undertakings including time-series information or regular language handling. Not at all like customary feedforward brain organizations, RNNs have associations that structure cycles, permitting them to keep a memory of past data sources. This memory empowers RNNs to catch conditions and connections inside successive information.

Move Learning:

Move learning is a procedure inside AI that use pre-prepared models for new, related undertakings. Rather than preparing a model without any preparation for each new errand, move learning includes utilizing a model prepared on an enormous dataset for a general undertaking and calibrating it on a more modest dataset for a particular assignment. This approach is especially beneficial when marked information for a particular undertaking is restricted.

Information and Component Designing:

The quality and variety of information assume an essential part in the progress of AI and profound learning models. Information preprocessing and include designing include errands like cleaning, normalizing, and changing information to improve its appropriateness for model preparation. Include designing spotlights on choosing or making pertinent elements that add to the prescient force of the model.

Difficulties and Contemplations:

Regardless of their extraordinary capacities, AI and profound learning face difficulties and contemplations. One critical test is the requirement for huge, marked datasets for viable preparation. Predispositions present in preparing information can bring about one-sided models, raising moral worries. Model interpretability is another test, particularly in complex profound learning models, where understanding the dynamic cycle is non-minor.

Interdisciplinary Nature:

AI and profound learning typify an interdisciplinary methodology, drawing from software engineering, insights, science, and area explicit information. The collaboration between these disciplines adds to the all encompassing comprehension and progression of smart frameworks. The cooperative endeavors of specialists, information researchers, and space specialists are fundamental for pushing the limits of what is feasible.

Applications Across Businesses:

The utilizations of AI and profound learning length different enterprises, introducing another period of advancement and effectiveness. In medical care, AI helps with clinical picture examination, diagnostics, and customized therapy plans. In finance, calculations controlled by AI enhance exchanging procedures, identify misrepresentation, and evaluate risk. Producing benefits from prescient support and quality control empowered by AI. Regular language handling methods upgrade remote helpers, language interpretation, and opinion investigation.

Future Patterns:

The fate of AI and profound learning holds energizing prospects. Proceeded with progressions in model designs, advancement procedures, and equipment abilities are expected. Logical simulated intelligence, meaning to make complex models more interpretable, is acquiring noticeable quality. Combined realizing, where models are prepared across decentralized gadgets while safeguarding security, addresses worries about incorporated information capacity. Quantum registering, with its capability to deal with huge datasets and perform complex calculations, presents fascinating possibilities for the fate of man-made intelligence.

1.2 Neural Networks and Algorithms

Brain organizations and calculations are essential parts of computerized reasoning, filling in as the spine for some applications and frameworks that display canny way of behaving. Brain organizations, enlivened by the design and working of the human cerebrum, structure the groundwork of AI and profound learning, while calculations give the efficient and procedural directions that empower PCs to perform explicit errands. As we dive into the complexities of brain organizations and calculations, we uncover the components that drive man-made reasoning forward.

Brain Organizations:

Brain networks are computational models intended to copy the interconnected construction of neurons in the human cerebrum. Containing layers of hubs, or fake neurons, these organizations cycle data in a way that empowers them to learn and simply decide. The fundamental structure block is the perceptron, a solitary layer brain network that gets input, applies loads to that info, totals the weighted data sources, and goes the outcome through an enactment capability to create a result.

Layers and Models:

Brain networks commonly comprise of an info layer, at least one secret layers, and a result layer.

The associations between hubs have related loads, and during preparing, these loads are changed in view of the blunder between the anticipated result and the genuine result. The profundity and construction of brain networks add to their capacity to learn complex examples and progressive portrayals of information.

Initiation Capabilities:

Enactment capabilities assume an essential part in brain networks by acquainting non-linearities with the model. Normal initiation capabilities incorporate the sigmoid, exaggerated digression (tanh), and redressed direct unit (ReLU). These capabilities empower brain organizations to catch non-straight connections inside information, permitting them to address and gain from complex examples.

Preparing and Backpropagation:

Preparing a brain network includes giving it named information, changing the loads in view of the blunder, and rehashing this cycle until the model precisely maps contributions to yields. Backpropagation is a key calculation utilized in this preparing system. It includes registering the slope of the blunder concerning the loads and changing the loads the other way of the angle. This iterative advancement process refines the brain organization's capacity to make exact expectations.

Convolutional Brain Organizations (CNNs):

Convolutional Brain Organizations (CNNs) are specific brain network structures intended for handling and investigating visual information, like pictures and recordings. CNNs utilize convolutional layers that apply channels to enter information, catching spatial orders of highlights. This progressive methodology permits CNNs to consequently learn and perceive designs in pictures, making them exceptionally compelling in errands like picture acknowledgment and article discovery.

Repetitive Brain Organizations (RNNs):

Intermittent Brain Organizations (RNNs) are intended to deal with successive information, making them appropriate for errands including time-series information or regular language handling. Not at all like feedforward brain organizations, RNNs have associations that structure cycles, permitting them to keep a memory of past sources of info. This memory empowers RNNs to catch conditions and connections inside consecutive information, making them compelling in undertakings, for example, discourse acknowledgment and language displaying.

Long Transient Memory (LSTM) Organizations:

LSTM networks are a sort of RNN intended to address the difficulties of catching long haul conditions in successive information. LSTMs present specific memory cells and gating components that control the progression of data through the organization. This engineering empowers LSTMs to specifically hold and fail to remember data overstretched arrangements, making them especially powerful in assignments where worldly conditions are significant.

Generative Ill-disposed Organizations (GANs):

Generative Ill-disposed Organizations (GANs) address a class of brain networks acquainted with create new information tests that look like a given dataset. GANs comprise of a generator network that makes manufactured information and a discriminator network that assesses the validness of the created tests. The exchange between the generator and discriminator in a serious setting prompts the age of reasonable and different information, making GANs important in errands, for example, picture age and style move.

Calculations:

Calculations, with regards to man-made brainpower, are bit by bit techniques or sets of rules for tackling explicit issues or performing assignments. While brain networks encapsulate the learning and dynamic abilities, calculations give the organized philosophy to preparing models, improving cycles, and making expectations. They are the consistent underpinnings that guide the orderly execution of assignments.

Directed Learning Calculations:

In administered realizing, where models are prepared on marked information, different calculations fill unmistakable needs. Straight relapse is utilized for anticipating persistent qualities, while choice trees and irregular timberlands succeed in arrangement errands. Support Vector Machines (SVMs) are successful for both grouping and relapse, and k-Closest Neighbors (k-NN) depends on vicinity based independent direction. The decision of calculation relies upon the idea of the issue and the attributes of the information.

Solo Learning Calculations:

Solo learning calculations work on unlabeled information, intending to reveal stowed away examples and designs. K-Means bunching bunches comparative information focuses together in view of highlights, while progressive grouping organizes information in a tree-like design. Head Part Examination (PCA) and t-Conveyed Stochastic Neighbor Implanting (t-SNE) are dimensionality decrease calculations that improve on complex datasets, making them more sensible for investigation.

Support Learning Calculations:

Support learning calculations guide specialists in learning ideal procedures through association with a climate. Q-Learning is a famous calculation for learning values related with state-activity matches, while Profound Q Organizations (DQN) influence profound figuring out how to deal with complex undertakings. Strategy Angle techniques straightforwardly streamline arrangements for direction. The mix of investigation and abuse in support learning calculations permits specialists to learn compelling systems over the long run.

Hereditary Calculations:

Hereditary calculations draw motivation from the course of regular determination to upgrade answers for complex issues. These calculations develop a populace of expected arrangements through determination, hybrid, and change, emulating the standards of natural advancement. Hereditary calculations are especially helpful in advancement issues where the pursuit space is tremendous and complex.

Algorithmic Intricacy:

Algorithmic intricacy, frequently communicated utilizing Enormous O documentation, measures the productivity of calculations regarding existence prerequisites. Productive calculations have lower existence intricacies, making them more adaptable for enormous datasets and constant applications. Understanding algorithmic intricacy is pivotal for advancing simulated intelligence frameworks and guaranteeing their functional feasibility.

Exchange Between Brain Organizations and Calculations:

The collaboration between brain organizations and calculations is clear in the preparation and advancement processes. Calculations like stochastic angle drop (SGD) and its variations, similar to Adam and RMSprop, guide the iterative change of loads in brain networks during preparing. These improvement calculations assume an essential part in calibrating models and guaranteeing union to ideal arrangements.

Difficulties and Contemplations:

Both brain organizations and calculations face difficulties and moral contemplations. Brain organizations might experience issues, for example, overfitting, where models perform well on preparing information however battle with new information, and evaporating or detonating slopes, which influence the steadiness of preparing. Moral contemplations include tending to predispositions in calculations, guaranteeing decency, and relieving the unseen side-effects of computer based intelligence frameworks.

1.3 Data, Big Data, and AI

The harmonious connection between information, huge information, and man-made reasoning (simulated intelligence) is at the center of the extraordinary abilities we observer in the area of innovation today. Information fills in as the soul of computer based intelligence, and the appearance of large information advancements has pushed the capacities of artificial intelligence frameworks to extraordinary levels. As we investigate the perplexing associations between information, huge information, and man-made intelligence, obviously the powerful usage of immense datasets is central to the turn of events and arrangement of wise frameworks.

Information:

Information, in its rawest structure, addresses the data that man-made intelligence frameworks cycle to decide, learn designs, and create bits of knowledge. This data can take different structures, including text, numbers, pictures, recordings, and that's just the beginning. The quality and amount of information significantly influence the exhibition and precision of artificial intelligence models. Information can be sorted as organized, semi-organized, or unstructured, contingent upon its configuration and association.

Organized Information:

Organized information is exceptionally coordinated and fits conveniently into social data sets. It is portrayed by a predefined outline, making it effectively accessible and analyzable. Instances of organized information incorporate calculation sheets, SQL data sets, and plain datasets.

Semi-Organized Information:

Semi-organized information misses the mark on severe association of organized information yet has some degree of design, frequently as labels, names, or progressive systems. Normal models incorporate JSON and XML records, which give a level of adaptability in addressing connections between information components.

Unstructured Information:

Unstructured information comes up short on predefined information model and isn't coordinated in an even or data set structure. This class incorporates text archives, pictures, sound documents, and video content. Breaking down unstructured information requires particular procedures, for example, regular language handling (NLP) for text or PC vision for pictures.

The Job of Information in simulated intelligence:

Information is the foundation of simulated intelligence, giving the preparation material important to AI calculations to recognize designs, make expectations, and perform assignments. In administered learning, models are prepared on marked datasets, where the information is matched with comparing yield names. Solo learning calculations, then again, break down unlabeled information to reveal examples and connections without unequivocal direction.

Preparing Information:

The nature of preparing information altogether impacts the exhibition of artificial intelligence models. All around named, various, and delegate datasets add to the model's capacity to sum up and make exact expectations on new, inconspicuous information. Moral contemplations with respect to the source and predispositions in preparing information are essential to building fair and unprejudiced simulated intelligence frameworks.

Testing and Approval Information:

Separate datasets for testing and approval are fundamental for surveying the speculation capacity of simulated intelligence models. Testing datasets assess the model's presentation on information it has not seen during preparing, while approval datasets help tweak hyperparameters and forestall overfitting.

The Difficulties of Information Quality:

Guaranteeing the nature of information is a constant test in manmade intelligence. Fragmented, erroneous, or one-sided information can prompt defective models and questionable forecasts. Information cleaning, preprocessing, and approval are critical stages in tending to these difficulties, guaranteeing that the information utilized for preparing and testing is of top notch.

Large Information:

Large information alludes to the monstrous volumes of information that surpass the limit of conventional information handling frameworks. The three Versus — Volume, Speed, and Assortment — describe large information. Volume alludes to the sheer size of information, Speed addresses the speed at which information is produced and handled, and Assortment incorporates the different sorts and wellsprings of information.

Volume:

The volume of information created in the advanced age is faltering, with organizations, online entertainment, sensors, and different sources delivering an exceptional measure of data. Large information advances are intended to productively deal with this enormous volume.

Speed:

The speed at which information is created and handled is one more principal quality of large information. Continuous information handling, frequently expected for applications like monetary exchanges, web-based entertainment associations, and sensor information from the Web of Things (IoT), requests progressed handling abilities.

Assortment:

Large information comes in different structures, including organized, semi-organized, and unstructured information. The range of information sources, like text, pictures, recordings, and sensor information, requires adaptable and versatile handling techniques.

Enormous Information Innovations:

A few innovations have arisen to handle the difficulties presented by enormous information. Appropriated figuring structures like Apache Hadoop and Apache Flash empower the equal handling of enormous datasets across groups of PCs.

NoSQL data sets, like MongoDB and Cassandra, give versatile capacity answers for assorted information types. Information lakes, which store information in its crude configuration, work with the capacity and examination of tremendous measures of data.

The Transaction Between Enormous Information and computer based intelligence:

Huge information and man-made intelligence are commonly supporting. Huge information gives the natural substance — enormous, various datasets — essential for preparing and refining man-made intelligence models. At the same time, simulated intelligence improves the examination of enormous information via mechanizing undertakings, recognizing designs, and extricating significant bits of knowledge at a scale that would be unfeasible for human investigators.

Information Handling:

Huge information innovations process tremendous measures of information effectively, empowering computer based intelligence calculations to work on enormous datasets. This versatility is critical for applications, for example, AI, where models benefit from preparing on broad and various information.

Continuous Investigation:

The speed of enormous information handling lines up with the requirement for continuous examination in man-made intelligence applications. Frameworks that require prompt reactions, like extortion discovery, proposal motors, and independent vehicles, influence huge information advances to process and examine information progressively.

Improved Bits of knowledge:

Enormous information improves the profundity and expansiveness of experiences got from simulated intelligence. The range of information sources — text, pictures, web-based entertainment communications — gives a comprehensive view, enhancing the information simulated intelligence models secure during preparing and working on their capacity to go with informed choices.

Difficulties of Huge Information in man-made intelligence:

While enormous information enhances the abilities of simulated intelligence, it additionally presents difficulties. Overseeing and putting away monstrous datasets request versatile framework, and handling these datasets requires complex calculations and conveyed frameworks. Security concerns and moral contemplations become more articulated as the size of information assortment and examination develops.

Protection and Security:

Huge information frequently contains delicate data, raising worries about protection and security. Finding some kind of harmony between utilizing significant information and safeguarding individual security is a basic thought in the turn of events and sending of computer based intelligence frameworks.

Moral Utilization of Information:

The moral utilization of huge information in man-made intelligence includes tending to predispositions present in enormous datasets, guaranteeing reasonableness in model expectations, and keeping away from potentially negative results. Straightforwardness in how information is gathered, handled, and utilized is fundamental for building trust in man-made intelligence frameworks.

The Fate of Information, Enormous Information, and artificial intelligence:

The direction of information, large information, and computer based intelligence focuses towards a future where smart frameworks become significantly more vital to our regular routines. As information proceeds to multiply and huge information innovations advance, man-made intelligence will additionally tackle the force of immense datasets to push the limits of what is reachable.

Progressions in computer based intelligence Models:

The combination of huge information will add to the refinement and improvement of man-made intelligence models. Future models will probably turn out to be more complex, fit for taking care of different information types, and addressing difficulties connected with interpretability and inclination.

Artificial intelligence in Edge Figuring:

The mix of man-made intelligence with edge figuring, where information handling happens nearer to the information source as opposed to in concentrated server farms, will turn out to be more common. This approach is especially important for applications that require low dormancy, like independent vehicles and IoT gadgets.

Mindful simulated intelligence:

The mindful and moral utilization of information in simulated intelligence will keep on acquiring unmistakable quality. Stricter guidelines, expanded mindfulness, and progressions in logical simulated intelligence will add to guaranteeing that man-made intelligence frameworks are created and sent in light of moral contemplations.

Chapter 2

AI in Industries: A Comprehensive Overview

Man-made consciousness (simulated intelligence) has arisen as a groundbreaking power across different enterprises, reshaping processes, upgrading productivity, and opening additional opportunities. From medical care to fund, assembling to retail, the joining of artificial intelligence innovations has prompted earth shattering headways. In this far reaching outline, we dig into the assorted uses of man-made intelligence in key ventures, investigating the manners by which shrewd frameworks are changing tasks, navigation, and development.

Medical care:

In the medical services industry, artificial intelligence is taking critical steps, adding to further developed diagnostics, customized therapy designs, and improved patient consideration. AI calculations dissect clinical pictures, like X beams and X-rays, with high precision, supporting the early identification of illnesses like malignant growth. Normal Language Handling (NLP) empowers the extraction of significant experiences from electronic wellbeing records, working with better clinical choice help.

Prescient examination models help with determining patient results and improving medical clinic asset allotment. Chatbots and virtual wellbeing partners fueled by artificial intelligence improve patient commitment and give continuous data.

Finance:

Artificial intelligence is reshaping the monetary scene via robotizing assignments, upgrading risk the board, and streamlining client encounters. Algorithmic exchanging depends on simulated intelligence calculations to break down market drifts and execute exchanges at speeds unreachable by human merchants. Misrepresentation identification frameworks influence AI to distinguish strange examples and oddities in monetary exchanges, supporting security. Simulated intelligence driven chatbots give customized monetary guidance, while robo-counselors computerize speculation portfolio the board. Regular language handling supports feeling examination of monetary news, assisting brokers with pursuing informed choices.

Producing:

In assembling, computer based intelligence advancements are driving the time of Industry 4.0, described by shrewd production lines and mechanized processes. Computer based intelligence controlled prescient upkeep investigates hardware information to expect likely disappointments, limiting margin time and expanding functional proficiency. PC vision frameworks investigate and guarantee the nature of items on the creation line. Cooperative robots, or cobots, furnished with simulated intelligence capacities work close by human administrators to smooth out assignments. Production network streamlining, request guaging, and stock administration benefit from artificial intelligence driven experiences, upgrading in general effectiveness.

Retail:

The retail area is going through a change with man-made intelligence applications improving client encounters, enhancing supply chains, and customizing promoting methodologies. Proposal motors, controlled by AI, break down client inclinations and ways of behaving to recommend customized items and administrations. PC vision in retail incorporates clerk less stores, brilliant racks, and facial acknowledgment for customized in-store encounters. Man-made intelligence driven chatbots help clients, handle requests, and work with consistent exchanges. Request guaging and stock administration benefit from prescient investigation, limiting stockouts and overload circumstances.

Broadcast communications:

In the broadcast communications industry, man-made intelligence is assuming a critical part in network improvement, client care, and extortion recognition. Prescient investigation models expect network disappointments and proactively advance execution.

Artificial intelligence driven chatbots and remote helpers improve client care by offering continuous help, investigating, and record the board. Normal language handling helps with examining client input and feelings, empowering telecom organizations to further develop administrations and address issues quickly. Artificial intelligence calculations likewise add to misrepresentation discovery by recognizing uncommon examples in call information records and organization action.

Transportation and Operations:

Computer based intelligence is reforming transportation and co-ordinated factors, upgrading course enhancement, prescient support, and wellbeing. Independent vehicles, fueled by simulated intelligence calculations and sensors, are being created for both traveler and cargo transport, promising superior security and productivity. Prescient support models examine information from sensors on vehicles and gear, limiting free time and decreasing upkeep costs. Man-made intelligence driven course enhancement thinks about ongoing traffic information, atmospheric conditions, and different variables to upgrade conveyance plans. Production network perceivability and request anticipating benefit from simulated intelligence examination, guaranteeing proficient and responsive strategies activities.

Energy:

In the energy area, man-made intelligence is driving headways in environmentally friendly power, lattice the board, and prescient upkeep. Artificial intelligence calculations enhance the activity and upkeep of sustainable power sources like sunlight based and wind ranches, further developing energy yield. Shrewd matrix the executives frameworks use computer based intelligence to adjust organic market, improve network versatility, and coordinate circulated energy assets. Prescient upkeep models investigate information from sensors and gear to expect disappointments, limiting personal time and decreasing support costs. Simulated intelligence likewise assumes a part in energy proficiency by upgrading utilization designs and recognizing regions for development.

Schooling:

Simulated intelligence applications in schooling are changing opportunities for growth, customizing training, and improving regulatory cycles. Versatile learning stages use simulated intelligence calculations to fit instructive substance to individual understudies' necessities and learning styles. Canny mentoring frameworks give constant criticism and backing to understudies. Normal language handling supports mechanized reviewing and input, saving instructors time. Chatbots help understudies with requests and authoritative undertakings. Prescient investigation models assist instructive establishments with recognizing in danger understudies and execute mediations to further develop degrees of consistency.

Farming:

In agribusiness, simulated intelligence advances are driving accuracy cultivating, crop observing, and yield enhancement. Drones furnished with PC vision and simulated intelligence dissect crop wellbeing, distinguish sicknesses, and evaluate the requirement for water system. Computer based intelligence driven sensors gather information on soil quality and dampness levels, empowering ranchers to arrive at informed conclusions about planting and collecting. Prescient investigation models gauge crop yields and assist with improving asset distribution.

Advanced mechanics and independent vehicles are used for undertakings like planting, collecting, and observing.

Diversion and Media:

Simulated intelligence is upsetting the amusement and media industry by improving substance creation, suggestion frameworks, and client encounters. Content proposal calculations use AI to investigate client inclinations and ways of behaving, giving customized ideas to motion pictures, music, and articles. Simulated intelligence driven content creation incorporates the age of craftsmanship, music, and in any event, composing. Virtual and increased reality encounters are improved by man-made intelligence calculations that adjust content in view of client associations. Regular language handling is utilized in feeling examination of client surveys and virtual entertainment, offering significant experiences for content makers and advertisers.

Difficulties and Contemplations:

While the incorporation of simulated intelligence across ventures achieves various advantages, it additionally presents difficulties and moral contemplations. Predisposition in simulated intelligence calculations, information security concerns, and the potential for work dislodging are issues that require cautious thought. Finding some kind of harmony among advancement and mindful computer based intelligence improvement is essential to guaranteeing the positive effect of these innovations on society.

2.1 Healthcare and Medicine

In the domain of medical services and medication, the reconciliation of Man-made brainpower (computer based intelligence) is introducing another time of potential outcomes, offering creative answers for long-standing difficulties and fundamentally affecting patient consideration, diagnostics, and therapy systems. As we investigate the diverse utilizations of computer based intelligence in medical services, it becomes apparent that these advances are expanding existing practices as well as reforming the whole medical care biological system.

Diagnostics and Imaging:

Simulated intelligence has exhibited exceptional abilities in the field of clinical imaging, changing how sicknesses are analyzed and observed. AI calculations, especially those using convolutional brain organizations (CNNs), succeed in picture acknowledgment assignments.

In radiology, artificial intelligence aids the early discovery of anomalies in X-beams, X-rays, CT filters, and other imaging modalities. For example, simulated intelligence calculations can distinguish unobtrusive indications of infections like disease, giving radiologists important bits of knowledge and working on demonstrative precision. The reconciliation of computer based intelligence in clinical imaging facilitates the demonstrative cycle as well as adds to additional exact and dependable outcomes.

Prescient Investigation and Customized Medication:

Prescient examination, controlled by man-made intelligence, assumes a significant part in estimating patient results and individualizing treatment plans. By examining immense datasets, including electronic wellbeing records, genomic data, and constant patient checking information, simulated intelligence models can recognize designs and anticipate the probability of explicit clinical occasions. This permits medical services suppliers to proactively mediate, customize therapy techniques, and upgrade patient consideration. Customized medication, worked with by simulated intelligence, tailors mediations in light of a patient's remarkable hereditary cosmetics, way of life, and clinical history, expanding treatment viability and limiting unfriendly impacts.

Drug Disclosure and Advancement:

Simulated intelligence is reshaping the medication revelation and advancement process, altogether speeding up the distinguishing proof of potential medication competitors and decreasing the time and expenses related with putting up new treatments for sale to the public. AI models break down huge datasets, including genomic data, protein structures, and biomedical writing, to distinguish potential medication targets and foresee the viability of mixtures. This information driven approach improves the effectiveness of medication revelation, permitting specialists to zero in on the most encouraging competitors and increment the achievement pace of clinical preliminaries. Man-made intelligence likewise works with the reusing of existing medications for new signs, giving extra roads to remedial advancement.

Advanced mechanics and Careful Help:

In the domain of medical procedure, computer based intelligence driven advanced mechanics are altering strategies, offering improved accuracy, proficiency, and negligibly obtrusive methods. Careful robots, directed by computer based intelligence calculations, help specialists in complex undertakings, empowering more prominent precision and diminishing the gamble of human mistake. The da Vinci Careful Framework, for instance, is a mechanical stage that permits specialists to carry out many-sided methodology with upgraded skill and control. Simulated intelligence calculations can break down ongoing information during medical procedure, giving bits of knowledge to help specialists in direction and working on persistent results. The cooperative energy between human skill and man-made intelligence driven advanced mechanics is changing careful practices and growing the extent of what is feasible in the working room.

Virtual Wellbeing Collaborators and Telemedicine:

Simulated intelligence driven virtual wellbeing partners and telemedicine stages are reshaping the manner in which medical care administrations are conveyed and gotten to. Chatbots outfitted with regular language handling capacities offer prompt help, answer questions, and work with arrangement booking. These remote helpers improve patient commitment, give ideal data, and smooth out authoritative errands. Telemedicine stages influence artificial intelligence for distant patient observing, diagnostics, and meetings, crossing over geological boundaries and expanding admittance to medical care administrations. Especially pertinent in the midst of worldwide wellbeing emergencies, telemedicine upheld by simulated intelligence advancements guarantees progression of care and diminishes the weight on medical services frameworks.

Normal Language Handling (NLP) in Medical services Records:

Regular Language Handling (NLP) is changing the investigation and extraction of data from huge volumes of medical care records, including clinical notes, clinical writing, and patient accounts. NLP calculations can filter through unstructured literary information, extricating important bits of knowledge and examples that add to clinical choice help. This innovation smoothes out regulatory errands via robotizing documentation, coding, and charging processes. By changing unstructured text into organized information, NLP improves the interoperability of medical services frameworks, works with information sharing, and supports proof based medication.

Remote Checking and Wearable Innovation:

The joining of computer based intelligence in distant patient observing and wearable innovation has introduced another time of proactive medical services. Wearable gadgets furnished with sensors gather continuous information on indispensable signs, movement levels, and other wellbeing measurements. Computer based intelligence calculations examine this persistent stream of information, permitting medical services suppliers to screen patients from a distance, recognize peculiarities, and intercede depending on the situation. This proactive methodology is especially useful for patients with constant circumstances, empowering early intercession, lessening hospitalizations, and further developing by and large wellbeing results.

Challenges and Moral Contemplations:

In spite of the groundbreaking capability of man-made intelligence in medical care, a few difficulties and moral contemplations should be tended to. The understanding of simulated intelligence produced experiences requires cautious approval to guarantee precision and unwavering quality. The potential for predispositions in computer based intelligence calculations, especially with regards to segment and financial differences, requires continuous examination and relief methodologies. Protection concerns connected with the capacity and investigation of touchy wellbeing information request hearty safety efforts and consistence with administrative structures like HIPAA.

Interdisciplinary Joint effort and Preparing:

The effective joining of computer based intelligence in medical care requires interdisciplinary coordinated effort between PC researchers, medical services experts, ethicists, and policymakers. Cross-disciplinary preparation programs are fundamental to outfit medical services experts with the abilities expected to comprehend, decipher, and team up really with computer based intelligence innovations. The moral contemplations encompassing computer based intelligence in medical services request continuous conversations and the foundation of rules to guarantee mindful turn of events, sending, and utilization of these advances.

2.2 Diagnosis and Treatment

The convergence of Man-made brainpower (artificial intelligence) with medical services has altered the cycles of finding and therapy, offering remarkable accuracy, speed, and customized ways to deal with patient consideration. As we dig into the utilizations of man-made intelligence in these basic regions, it becomes apparent that the mix of wise advancements is reshaping clinical works on, working on clinical results, and rethinking the scene of medical services conveyance.

Demonstrative Progressions:

Artificial intelligence has arisen as a considerable partner in clinical diagnostics, enlarging the capacities of medical services experts and speeding up the recognizable proof of illnesses. In fields, for example, radiology, artificial intelligence fueled picture examination is changing the understanding of clinical imaging, including X-beams, X-rays, and CT checks. AI calculations, especially convolutional brain organizations (CNNs), succeed in recognizing unobtrusive anomalies and examples characteristic of illnesses, like cancers or breaks. The speed and exactness with which artificial intelligence can dissect clinical pictures smooth out the symptomatic cycle as well as add to early recognition, a vital calculate further developing treatment results.

Accuracy Medication and Biomarker Disclosure:

The coming of accuracy medication, worked with by man-made intelligence, denotes a change in outlook in treatment systems, creating some distance from one-size-fits-all ways to deal with customized mediations custom-made to individual patients. Man-made intelligence calculations dissect huge datasets, including genomic data, patient accounts, and treatment reactions, to distinguish biomarkers related with explicit infections. This data empowers medical care suppliers to anticipate how a patient will answer specific therapies, considering the choice of treatments that are probably going to be viable. Accuracy medication holds the commitment of expanding therapy viability while limiting secondary effects, introducing a period of designated and individualized clinical intercessions.

Clinical Choice Emotionally supportive networks:

Computer based intelligence driven clinical choice emotionally supportive networks (CDSS) assume a significant part in helping medical services experts by giving proof based bits of knowledge, therapy proposals, and important data at the place of care. These frameworks examine patient information, clinical writing, and best practices to offer constant direction to clinicians. CDSS lessens symptomatic blunders, upholds treatment arranging, and guarantees that medical care suppliers approach the most recent examination and clinical rules. The coordination of man-made intelligence in clinical dynamic upgrades the nature of care, advances normalization, and adds to better persistent results.

Regular Language Handling in Electronic Wellbeing Records:

The huge measures of unstructured information inside electronic wellbeing records (EHRs) present a test for powerful investigation and use. Regular Language Handling (NLP), a subset of computer based intelligence, addresses this test by extricating significant data from free-text clinical notes, reports, and other printed information. NLP calculations can recognize applicable insights regarding patient circumstances, treatment plans, and results, changing unstructured text into organized, significant information. This smoothes out authoritative cycles as well as gives significant bits of knowledge to clinical exploration, quality improvement drives, and review examinations.

Virtual Wellbeing Aides in Tolerant Commitment:

Virtual wellbeing associates controlled by simulated intelligence are upgrading patient commitment and correspondence, adding to further developed wellbeing results and adherence to treatment plans. These insightful chatbots connect with patients, noting questions, giving drug updates, and offering support for ongoing illness the executives. Simulated intelligence driven remote helpers reach out past routine regulatory undertakings, encouraging a more customized and nonstop association among patients and medical services suppliers. This commitment adds to a comprehensive way to deal with patient consideration, advancing health, and forestalling expected difficulties.

Advanced mechanics in Medical procedure and Therapy Conveyance:

Man-made intelligence driven advanced mechanics are changing surgeries, empowering upgraded accuracy, negligibly intrusive procedures, and, surprisingly, far off medical procedures. Careful robots, directed by simulated intelligence calculations, can help or try and carry out specific techniques with more prominent precision and skill than customary strategies. The da Vinci Careful Framework, for instance, is generally utilized in techniques going from prostate medical procedure to cardiovascular medical procedure. Moreover, computer based intelligence fueled automated frameworks are being utilized in radiation treatment for malignant growth therapy, considering exceptionally designated and exact conveyance of restorative portions while limiting harm to encompassing solid tissues.

Drug Disclosure and Treatment Enhancement:

The reconciliation of man-made intelligence in drug revelation speeds up the recognizable proof of potential medication competitors and improves the advancement of treatment regimens. AI models investigate huge datasets, including atomic designs, natural pathways, and patient reactions, to foresee the adequacy and security of medication compounds. This information driven approach speeds up the medication improvement process, decreases expenses, and improves the probability of effective clinical preliminaries. Artificial intelligence additionally adds to treatment enhancement by dissecting continuous patient information, changing drug portions in view of individual reactions, and distinguishing possible antagonistic responses, consequently boosting treatment benefits.

Difficulties and Contemplations:

While the likely advantages of man-made intelligence in determination and treatment are tremendous, a few difficulties and contemplations should be addressed to guarantee dependable and compelling execution.

Interpretability and Reasonableness:

The "discovery" nature of some artificial intelligence calculations presents difficulties in understanding and deciphering their dynamic cycles. Guaranteeing the interpretability and reasonableness of artificial intelligence models is essential for acquiring the trust of medical services experts, patients, and administrative bodies.

Information Quality and Inclination:

The dependability of simulated intelligence driven experiences is dependent upon the quality and representativeness of the information utilized for preparing. Predispositions present in authentic datasets can be propagated in man-made intelligence models, possibly prompting variations in determination and treatment suggestions. Thorough information quality affirmation and predisposition relief procedures are fundamental for moral man-made intelligence applications in medical services.

Administrative Consistence and Protection:

Medical care information is exceptionally delicate, and the utilization of computer based intelligence in analysis and therapy should stick to rigid administrative structures, for example, the Health care coverage Versatility and Responsibility Act (HIPAA). Guaranteeing consistence with security guidelines and safeguarding patient information from unapproved access or abuse is a central concern.

Human-man-made intelligence Cooperation:

The fruitful mix of computer based intelligence in medical services requires compelling coordinated effort between simulated intelligence frameworks and human medical services experts.

Guaranteeing that artificial intelligence increases as opposed to replaces human mastery requires insightful plan, progressing preparing, and clear correspondence about the jobs of both simulated intelligence and human specialists.

2.3 Drug Discovery

The course of medication disclosure, a complex and asset escalated venture, has been essentially changed by the joining of Man-made reasoning (computer based intelligence) innovations. From the ID of potential medication contender to the streamlining of treatment regimens, simulated intelligence is assuming a vital part in speeding up the medication improvement pipeline, decreasing expenses, and improving the probability of fruitful clinical results.

Distinguishing proof of Medication Targets:

The principal significant stage in drug disclosure is the distinguishing proof of reasonable medication targets, frequently proteins or qualities related with a particular sickness. Artificial intelligence calculations, especially AI models, dissect huge datasets containing genomic data, protein structures, and organic pathways to recognize likely targets. This information driven approach permits specialists to focus on focuses with a higher probability of progress, smoothing out the underlying phases of medication revelation.

Prescient Investigation for Medication Adequacy:

Prescient examination, fueled by computer based intelligence, assumes a basic part in determining the viability of potential medication up-and-comers. AI models dissect different datasets, including sub-atomic designs, pharmacological properties, and verifiable clinical preliminary information, to foresee how a medication up-and-comer is probably going to act in human preliminaries. This information driven approach empowers scientists to focus on promising competitors, expanding the proficiency of the medication revelation interaction and diminishing the probability of late-stage disappointments.

Drug Reusing:

Man-made intelligence adds to medicate revelation by distinguishing novel up-and-comers as well as by reusing existing medications for new restorative signs. Drug reusing includes utilizing simulated intelligence calculations to break down tremendous datasets, including clinical preliminary information, electronic wellbeing records, and biomedical writing, to distinguish existing medications that might have possible applications in treating various sicknesses. This approach speeds up the advancement course of events, as reused drugs have proactively gone through wellbeing testing and may make known side impacts, smoothing out the administrative endorsement process.

Chemoinformatics and Atomic Plan:

In the domain of chemoinformatics, artificial intelligence supports the plan of novel medication particles with improved pharmacological properties. AI models break down synthetic designs, restricting affinities, and other sub-atomic properties to foresee the probability of a compound being a fruitful medication competitor. This information driven atomic plan approach empowers specialists to create speculations about new mixtures, altogether lessening the experimentation parts of customary medication improvement.

High-Throughput Screening:

Simulated intelligence advances, including mechanical technology and AI calculations, are instrumental in high-throughput screening (HTS) processes. HTS includes quickly testing enormous libraries of mixtures to recognize those with likely helpful impacts. Computerized mechanical frameworks, directed by simulated intelligence calculations, can perform large number of examinations in a negligible portion of the time it would take utilizing customary techniques. The reconciliation of artificial intelligence in HTS speeds up the distinguishing proof of promising mixtures and speeds up the beginning phases of medication disclosure.

Clinical Preliminary Enhancement:

When a potential medication competitor advances to clinical preliminaries, simulated intelligence keeps on assuming a significant part in streamlining preliminary plan and patient enlistment. Prescient investigation models break down verifiable clinical preliminary information to streamline preliminary conventions, including the choice of patient populaces, measurement levels, and endpoints. Artificial intelligence driven calculations likewise aid patient enrollment by recognizing reasonable up-and-comers in light of predefined rules, guaranteeing that preliminaries are directed effectively and with a higher probability of progress.

Constant Information Examination:

The appearance of ongoing information investigation controlled by computer based intelligence is changing how clinical preliminaries are directed. Computer based intelligence calculations investigate continuous patient information, including biomarkers, unfavorable occasions, and treatment reactions, taking into account versatile preliminary plans. This unique methodology empowers specialists to make constant changes in accordance with preliminary conventions in view of arising information, upgrading the effectiveness of clinical preliminaries and improving the probability of distinguishing significant treatment impacts.

Difficulties and Contemplations:

While the reconciliation of artificial intelligence in drug revelation achieves huge benefits, it isn't without difficulties and contemplations.

Information Quality and Inclination:

The dependability of man-made intelligence driven experiences in drug revelation depends vigorously on the quality and representativeness of the information utilized for preparing. Predispositions present in authentic datasets can be propagated in computer based intelligence models, possibly prompting differences in drug disclosure endeavors.

Guaranteeing thorough information quality affirmation and predisposition relief methodologies is fundamental for moral and successful simulated intelligence applications in drug disclosure.

Interpretability and Logic:

The interpretability and logic of man-made intelligence models are essential for acquiring the trust of analysts, administrative bodies, and the more extensive academic local area. Understanding how man-made intelligence calculations show up at explicit expectations or suggestions is fundamental for informed dynamic in drug revelation.

Administrative Consistence:

The administrative scene for artificial intelligence applications in drug disclosure is advancing. Guaranteeing consistence with administrative structures and norms is principal to the effective joining of simulated intelligence advancements into the medication improvement pipeline. Clear rules and cooperation among analysts and administrative bodies are fundamental for exploring this mind boggling scene.

Human-computer based intelligence Cooperation:

While simulated intelligence essentially expands drug disclosure processes, human aptitude stays crucial. Compelling cooperation between artificial intelligence frameworks and human scientists is vital for saddling the maximum capacity of these advancements. Coordinating man-made intelligence into existing work processes and guaranteeing that scientists can decipher and follow up on artificial intelligence created bits of knowledge are key contemplations.

2.4 Finance and Banking

The money and banking industry is going through a significant change with the combination of Man-made brainpower (computer based intelligence) innovations. From client connections to gamble with the executives and misrepresentation identification, simulated intelligence is reforming customary financial works on, offering expanded proficiency, upgraded direction, and further developed client encounters.

Client support and Commitment:

Computer based intelligence is reshaping client care in the money and banking area through the execution of remote helpers and chatbots. These clever frameworks influence Normal Language Handling (NLP) to comprehend and answer client questions and demands continuously. Remote helpers, for example, chatbots, offer moment help for routine requests, account data, and conditional exercises. This works on the effectiveness of client care as well as improves the general client experience by giving day in and day out help and lessening stand by times.

Customized Monetary Counsel:

Man-made intelligence driven robo-counsels are changing the scene of monetary warning administrations. These robotized stages use AI calculations to investigate client inclinations, risk resilience, and monetary objectives. Overwhelmingly of monetary information, robo-guides can create customized speculation proposals and portfolio systems. This democratization of monetary guidance gives clients open, financially savvy, and customized speculation arrangements, considering a more comprehensive way to deal with abundance the executives.

Credit Scoring and Chance Administration:

Simulated intelligence assumes a crucial part in credit scoring and hazard evaluation, empowering more precise forecasts of reliability and possible dangers. AI models dissect different information sources, including exchange history, social way of behaving, and elective informational indexes, to survey a person's or a business' credit risk. This approach permits monetary establishments to go with more educated loaning choices, growing admittance to credit for a more extensive scope of candidates and limiting the gamble of defaults.

Misrepresentation Recognition and Security:

In the fight against monetary misrepresentation, artificial intelligence advances are instrumental in identifying and forestalling dubious exercises. AI calculations break down designs in exchange information to recognize peculiarities that might demonstrate fake way of behaving. Computer based intelligence driven extortion discovery frameworks can adjust and develop to perceive new sorts of misrepresentation, giving a proactive and dynamic safeguard against digital dangers. This is significant for defending client resources and keeping up with the honesty of monetary exchanges in an undeniably digitized financial climate.

Algorithmic Exchanging and Market Investigation:

Artificial intelligence has changed the scene of monetary business sectors through the execution of algorithmic exchanging procedures. AI calculations dissect market information, news, and online entertainment feelings to make quick, information driven exchanging choices. High-recurrence exchanging (HFT) controlled by simulated intelligence can execute complex exchanging systems at speeds unreachable by human merchants. Also, artificial intelligence driven market examination adds to additional precise expectations of market patterns, helping financial backers in going with informed choices and overseeing portfolios successfully.

Against Illegal tax avoidance (AML) Consistence:

The money business faces rigid administrative prerequisites, especially in the domain of Against Illegal tax avoidance (AML) consistence. Simulated intelligence advances, including AI and example acknowledgment, improve AML endeavors via mechanizing the discovery of dubious exchanges and recognizing potential tax evasion exercises. The capacity of man-made intelligence frameworks to examine enormous datasets continuously fundamentally works on the effectiveness and exactness of AML consistence processes, guaranteeing monetary foundations stick to administrative guidelines and alleviate the dangers related with illegal monetary exercises.

Administrative Consistence and Detailing:

Exploring the intricate scene of administrative consistence is difficult for monetary organizations. Computer based intelligence assumes a vital part in robotizing consistence processes and guaranteeing adherence to developing administrative necessities. AI calculations investigate administrative changes, evaluate their effect on existing cycles, and mechanize the age of consistence reports. This upgrades the effectiveness of consistence endeavors as well as diminishes the gamble of blunders and resistance, at last adding to a more vigorous and straightforward monetary framework.

Information Security and Protection:

As monetary organizations handle immense measures of delicate client information, it is vital to guarantee information security and protection. Man-made intelligence advancements add to network protection endeavors by ceaselessly checking for likely dangers, distinguishing weaknesses, and answering security episodes progressively. AI calculations can identify designs demonstrative of digital assaults, giving a proactive protection against information breaks and unapproved access. The combination of man-made intelligence in network safety rehearses is significant for protecting client data and keeping up with trust in the computerized financial biological system.

Functional Proficiency and Cost Decrease:

Simulated intelligence driven computerization improves functional productivity in financial cycles, diminishing manual responsibility and related costs. Mechanical Interaction Computerization (RPA) mechanizes routine errands, for example, information passage, archive handling, and consistence checks. This permits banking experts to zero in on additional complex and worth added exercises, working on generally speaking efficiency. The execution of simulated intelligence advancements adds to cost decrease by smoothing out activities, limiting mistakes, and enhancing asset assignment.

Difficulties and Contemplations:

While the combination of artificial intelligence carries various advantages to the money and banking area, it additionally presents difficulties and contemplations that require cautious consideration.

Moral Utilization of simulated intelligence:

Guaranteeing the moral utilization of simulated intelligence in finance is fundamental, especially concerning issues like algorithmic predisposition and decency. Monetary organizations should focus on straightforwardness, reasonableness, and responsibility in their man-made intelligence applications to abstain from supporting existing predispositions and guarantee fair results for all clients.

Administrative and Lawful Consistence:

Exploring the administrative scene is really difficult for the money business. Monetary establishments should keep up to date with developing guidelines connected with the utilization of artificial intelligence, information security, and online protection. Consistence with these guidelines is basic to staying away from legitimate difficulties and keeping up with the trust of clients and administrative specialists.

Information Protection and Security Concerns:

As computer based intelligence applications in finance depend on huge measures of touchy client information, guaranteeing powerful information protection and safety efforts is of most extreme significance. Monetary establishments should major areas of strength for execute, secure information stockpiling practices, and extensive network safety methodologies to safeguard client data from unapproved access or breaks.

Human-computer based intelligence Joint effort:

While artificial intelligence advances upgrade productivity, human oversight stays vital, particularly in dynamic cycles. Finding some kind of harmony among mechanization and human aptitude is fundamental to guarantee dependable and moral utilization of man-made intelligence in finance. Human-man-made intelligence joint effort includes planning frameworks that enable human leaders with artificial intelligence created experiences while considering the moral ramifications of computerized navigation.

2.5 Algorithmic Trading

Algorithmic exchanging, frequently alluded to as algo exchanging, is a complex and innovation driven way to deal with monetary business sectors that depends on mechanized frameworks and calculations to execute exchanges with speed and accuracy. This type of exchanging has acquired massive prominence ongoing years, altering the elements of monetary business sectors and acquainting new intricacies with the exchanging scene.

Definition and Component:

At its center, algorithmic exchanging includes the utilization of PC calculations to execute exchanging procedures with insignificant human intercession. These calculations are modified to adhere to explicit arrangements of guidelines, considering different market pointers, cost developments, and other pertinent elements. The objective is to settle on exchanging choices in light of predefined models and execute orders at ideal costs.

The instruments of algorithmic exchanging can fluctuate, enveloping a great many systems. A few calculations center around taking advantage of transient market shortcomings, utilizing high-recurrence exchanging (HFT) strategies to profit by cost inconsistencies that might exist for just parts of a second. Others might utilize more mind boggling methodologies, for example, measurable exchange or pattern following, to catch more extensive market patterns and open doors.

Key Parts of Algorithmic Exchanging:

System Definition:

Prior to executing algorithmic exchanging, merchants or quantitative experts foster exchanging methodologies. These methodologies can be founded on different variables, including specialized markers, factual models, AI calculations, or a mix of these components. The objective is to characterize a bunch of decides that the calculation will follow to pursue exchanging choices.

Calculation Advancement:

When the exchanging procedure is planned, it is made an interpretation of into PC code to make the calculation. This includes programming the particular standards and conditions that the calculation will use to dissect market information and execute exchanges. The calculation ought to be intended to work progressively, handling data quickly to profit by market amazing open doors.

Market Information Examination:

Algorithmic exchanging depends intensely on the examination of market information. This remembers ongoing data for cost developments, exchanging volume, bid-ask spreads, and other pertinent measurements. The calculation processes this information to recognize examples, patterns, or abnormalities that line up with the predefined exchanging procedure.

Risk The executives:

Powerful gamble the board is a urgent part of algorithmic exchanging. Calculations integrate risk controls and position-measuring boundaries to oversee openness and forestall huge misfortunes. Risk the board calculations might incorporate stop-misfortune orders, position limits, and different systems to guarantee that the exchanging procedure lines up with the gamble resistance of the broker or asset.

Request Execution:

One of the essential benefits of algorithmic exchanging is its capacity to execute orders with excellent speed and accuracy. Calculations can consequently submit, change, or drop orders in light of economic situations. The objective is to accomplish the most ideal execution costs while limiting business sector effect and exchange costs.

Benefits of Algorithmic Exchanging:

Speed and Effectiveness:

Algorithmic exchanging works at speeds impossible by human brokers. With the capacity to handle huge measures of information and execute exchanges milliseconds, calculations exploit temporary market valuable open doors and answer changing circumstances with unrivaled proficiency.

Disposal of Close to home Inclination:

Via mechanizing exchanging choices, algorithmic exchanging takes out profound inclinations that can affect human merchants. Calculations execute exchanges in view of predefined rules, without capitulating to dread, avarice, or different feelings that might impact human direction.

Broadening and Intricacy:

Calculations can deal with a large number of techniques at the same time, considering broadening across business sectors and instruments. In addition, algorithmic exchanging procedures can be exceptionally complicated, consolidating progressed numerical models and AI methods to adjust to changing economic situations.

Expanded Liquidity:

Algorithmic exchanging adds to advertise liquidity by giving consistent trade orders. This liquidity benefits other market members, making it simpler for merchants to execute huge orders without essentially influencing costs.

Backtesting and Streamlining:

Preceding arrangement, calculations go through broad backtesting utilizing authentic information to evaluate their exhibition. This permits brokers to upgrade systems, tweak boundaries, and assess the calculation's power under different economic situations.

Difficulties and Dangers:

Market Effect:

While algorithmic exchanging plans to limit market influence, the sheer volume of exchanges executed by calculations can, in specific circumstances, impact market costs.

Huge scope algorithmic exchanging exercises can possibly cause market interruptions or add to streak crashes.

Specialized Errors:

The dependence on innovation opens algorithmic exchanging to the gamble of specialized errors or framework disappointments. A breaking down calculation can prompt unseen side-effects, including huge monetary misfortunes. Defends and safeguards are fundamental to moderate such dangers.

Administrative Examination:

The quick development of algorithmic exchanging has drawn in administrative examination. Controllers are worried about the potential for market control, unjustifiable benefits, and the effect of algorithmic exchanging on market steadiness. Consistence with administrative systems is vital for members in algorithmic exchanging.

Over-Streamlining:

The most common way of backtesting and improving calculations can prompt overfitting, where the calculation performs well on verifiable information yet battles to adjust to new economic situations. Finding some kind of harmony between upgrading for verifiable execution and guaranteeing flexibility to changing business sectors is a critical test.

Network protection Dangers:

Algorithmic exchanging frameworks are helpless to network protection dangers, including hacking endeavors, information breaks, and other vindictive exercises. Strong network safety measures are basic to safeguard delicate exchanging calculations and guarantee the respectability of monetary business sectors.

The Fate of Algorithmic Exchanging:

The fate of algorithmic exchanging is probably going to be portrayed by proceeded with progressions in innovation, expanded utilization of AI and computerized reasoning, and an emphasis on tending to administrative worries. As innovation advances, calculations might turn out to be significantly more refined, integrating further layers of examination and adjusting to a consistently changing monetary scene. The continuous cooperation between monetary foundations, technologists, and controllers will assume a pivotal part in molding the fate of algorithmic exchanging and guaranteeing its capable and viable joining into worldwide monetary business sectors.

2.6 Fraud Detection

Extortion recognition, a basic part of chance administration in different enterprises, has developed essentially with the coordination of refined advancements, especially Computerized reasoning (man-made intelligence). As organizations progressively work in a computerized scene, the gamble of fake exercises has developed, making the execution of vigorous misrepresentation location frameworks basic.

Customary Techniques versus Simulated intelligence in Extortion Discovery:

Customary extortion discovery techniques frequently depend on rule-based frameworks and predefined edges to signal possibly dubious exercises. While these frameworks have been viable somewhat, they might miss the mark on flexibility and precision expected to battle the advancing strategies of fraudsters. Enter man-made intelligence controlled misrepresentation location, which use progressed calculations, AI, and information investigation to improve the capacity to identify fake examples and irregularities.

AI Calculations:

AI is a foundation of man-made intelligence controlled misrepresentation discovery. These calculations gain from verifiable information, persistently working on their capacity to recognize designs demonstrative of false way of behaving. Directed learning models can be prepared on named datasets containing instances of both genuine and deceitful exchanges, permitting the calculation to perceive unobtrusive examples that might evade rule-based frameworks.

Peculiarity Location:

Oddity recognition is a predominant methodology in simulated intelligence based misrepresentation discovery. This technique includes making a standard of typical way of behaving and hailing exercises that veer off from this benchmark as possibly deceitful. AI models can independently adjust to changes in designs, distinguishing peculiarities that might connote fake exercises without the requirement for express rule-setting.

Social Investigation:

Computer based intelligence empowers the investigation of client conduct to distinguish deviations from laid out designs. This incorporates examining how clients communicate with advanced stages, their run of the mill exchange narratives, and the gadgets they use. Conduct examination can distinguish surprising examples, like abrupt changes in spending conduct or getting to accounts from new areas, setting off cautions for additional examination.

Constant Investigation:

One of the critical benefits of simulated intelligence in extortion location is its capacity to process and examine huge measures of information progressively. Conventional frameworks frequently work on clump handling, which might prompt deferred location.

Simulated intelligence frameworks, then again, can survey exchanges, exercises, or connections promptly, taking into consideration quick recognizable proof and reaction to expected false occasions.

Reconciliation of artificial intelligence in Different Businesses:

The utilization of artificial intelligence in misrepresentation identification traverses different businesses, including banking and money, web based business, medical services, and protection.

Banking and Money: In the monetary area, computer based intelligence is instrumental in distinguishing false exchanges, account takeovers, and unapproved access. AI models examine conditional information, login designs, and verifiable ways of behaving to identify oddities and banner possibly false exercises. The speed at which computer based intelligence processes information is especially significant in forestalling monetary misfortunes because of false exchanges.

Internet business: Online retailers face the steady test of fighting false exercises, like installment misrepresentation, account takeover, and phony audits. Computer based intelligence calculations dissect client conduct, exchange chronicles, and different relevant variables to distinguish dubious exercises progressively, improving the security of online exchanges.

Medical care: The medical services industry is defenseless against different types of extortion, including protection misrepresentation and wholesale fraud. Computer based intelligence driven extortion discovery frameworks investigate claims information, patient accounts, and charging examples to recognize inconsistencies or peculiarities that might show fake exercises. This assists medical services associations with alleviating monetary misfortunes and guarantee the uprightness of patient records.

Insurance: In the protection area, extortion can appear in different ways, including bogus cases, payment avoidance, or fraud. Man-made intelligence fueled frameworks break down verifiable information and examples to recognize possibly deceitful cases, empowering safety net providers to go to proactive lengths to forestall misfortunes and keep up with the validity of their activities.

Difficulties and Contemplations:

While man-made intelligence has essentially improved extortion recognition capacities, it accompanies its own arrangement of difficulties and contemplations.

Information Quality and Inclination: The viability of computer based intelligence models relies upon the quality and representativeness of the information utilized for preparing. Predispositions present in authentic information might be propagated in AI models, prompting slanted results. Guaranteeing assorted and delegate datasets is vital to limiting predisposition in extortion identification frameworks.

Ill-disposed Assaults: Fraudsters might endeavor to beguile simulated intelligence frameworks by taking advantage of weaknesses or presenting manipulative examples. Ill-disposed assaults include creating contributions to delude AI models. Carrying out hearty safety efforts and continuous observing are fundamental to alleviate the gamble of ill-disposed assaults.

Interpretability and Reasonableness: The "discovery" nature of some computer based intelligence calculations raises worries about interpretability and logic. Understanding how man-made intelligence frameworks come to explicit end results is critical for acquiring the trust of clients, examiners, and administrative bodies. Guaranteeing straightforwardness in the dynamic cycle is fundamental for responsibility.

Administrative Consistence: Adherence to administrative structures is vital in the sending of man-made intelligence in extortion location, particularly in enterprises with severe consistence necessities.

Monetary foundations and medical services suppliers should explore administrative scenes to guarantee that their computer based intelligence controlled extortion location frameworks conform to industry guidelines and lawful structures.

2.7 Manufacturing and Automation

The assembling business is going through a progressive change with the broad reception of computerization innovations. The mix of computerization into assembling processes has achieved critical enhancements in effectiveness, accuracy, and generally speaking efficiency. This shift towards computerization addresses a basic change in the manner merchandise are delivered, affecting different features of the assembling scene.

Modern Mechanical technology and Computerization:

One of the key components driving the change in assembling is the arrangement of modern advanced mechanics. These refined machines are intended to perform undertakings generally did by human specialists, going from gathering and welding to material taking care of and bundling. Modern robots, furnished with sensors and high level control frameworks, can work with accuracy and speed, improving the consistency and nature of made items.

Advantages of Mechanization in Assembling:

The reception of mechanization in assembling offers a few convincing benefits. Right off the bat, robotization increments productivity by decreasing creation process durations and limiting blunders. Robots can work constantly without the requirement for breaks or moves, prompting a huge expansion in general creation yield. Moreover, robotization upgrades item quality and consistency by dispensing with varieties presented by human elements.

Besides, mechanization adds to cost reserve funds over the long haul. While the underlying interest in mechanization innovation can be significant, the continuous functional expenses are much of the time lower than keeping a labor force. In addition, the decreased wiggle room and waste, combined with expanded throughput, bring about better asset usage and by and large expense adequacy.

Thirdly, mechanization tends to work deficiencies and ability holes. In numerous businesses, there is a developing test of tracking down talented work to perform explicit undertakings. Robotization mitigates this test by taking over tedious and work serious cycles, permitting human specialists to zero in on additional perplexing errands that require decisive reasoning and critical thinking abilities.

Difficulties and Contemplations:

Notwithstanding, the inescapable reception of mechanization additionally presents difficulties and contemplations. The relocation of human specialists by machines raises worries about employment cutback and the requirement for upskilling the labor force. Critical for makers to execute systems work with the change of laborers into jobs that supplement robotization, underlining undertakings that require inventiveness, versatility, and high level specialized abilities.

One more test is the high starting expense of carrying out robotization frameworks. While the drawn out benefits are obvious, a few producers might confront monetary boundaries in embracing computerization innovation. States, industry affiliations, and monetary establishments assume a part in boosting and supporting organizations in their change towards mechanization.

The joining of robotization additionally requires strong network protection measures. As assembling frameworks become progressively interconnected through the Web of Things (IoT) and Industry 4.0 drives, the gamble of digital dangers and assaults on basic foundation develops. Makers should focus on network safety to shield delicate information, protected innovation, and keep up with the trustworthiness of robotized processes.

Future Patterns and Developments:

Looking forward, the eventual fate of assembling and computerization is set apart by continuous progressions and developments. Man-made reasoning (simulated intelligence) is turning out to be more common in assembling, empowering machines to gain from information, decide, and improve processes independently. Cooperative robots, or cobots, are arising as a pattern, working close by human administrators to improve productivity and adaptability in assembling conditions.

Additionally, the idea of the shrewd industrial facility, portrayed by interconnected frameworks and ongoing information trade, is building up some momentum. This Industry 4.0 worldview use innovations, for example, IoT, distributed computing, and large information investigation to make more dexterous and responsive assembling biological systems.

2.8 Robotics and Smart Factories

The union of mechanical technology and savvy processing plants is introducing another period of modern mechanization, where insightful machines work consistently close by human administrators to make more effective, adaptable, and responsive assembling conditions. Mechanical technology assumes an essential part in changing conventional processing plants into savvy production lines, adding to improved efficiency, quality, and by and large functional greatness.

Modern Mechanical technology in Assembling:

Modern robots are at the front of the mechanization upset in assembling. These robots, furnished with cutting edge sensors, actuators, and programming capacities, can play out a different scope of errands across different enterprises. From gathering and welding to material taking care of and examination, modern robots bring accuracy, speed, and consistency to assembling processes.

The adaptability of modern robots is a key resource, permitting them to adjust to various errands and item varieties with negligible reinventing. This flexibility makes them significant resources in ventures with different product offerings and changing creation prerequisites. Cooperative robots, or cobots, address a subset of modern robots intended to work securely close by human administrators, working with close coordinated effort and upgrading generally speaking proficiency.

Brilliant Manufacturing plants and Industry 4.0:

The idea of brilliant production lines is firmly connected with Industry 4.0, a worldview that use computerized innovations to make interconnected and savvy fabricating frameworks.

In a brilliant production line, information turns into a focal resource, and machines speak with one another progressively. This network is accomplished through the combination of advancements like the Web of Things (IoT), distributed computing, and computerized reasoning.

Brilliant production lines empower a more comprehensive and information driven way to deal with assembling. Sensors implanted in machines gather information on different parts of the creation cycle, from machine execution to item quality. This information is then dissected continuously, giving bits of knowledge that can be utilized to upgrade creation, anticipate support needs, and pursue informed choices to improve generally speaking productivity.

Advantages of Mechanical technology and Brilliant Processing plants:

The mix of mechanical technology and savvy processing plant advancements yields a few huge advantages for makers. There, right off the bat, is an undeniable improvement in efficiency. Modern robots can work all day, every day, decreasing process durations and expanding throughput. Brilliant processing plants influence constant information examination to recognize bottlenecks, smooth out work processes, and advance asset distribution, further upgrading efficiency.

Furthermore, there is a significant improvement in quality and consistency. The accuracy and repeatability of modern robots add to the development of great items with negligible deformities. Brilliant manufacturing plants make this a stride further by utilizing information investigation to screen and control quality boundaries, guaranteeing that items meet or surpass rigid quality guidelines.

Thirdly, the coordinated effort between human laborers and robots in shrewd processing plants makes a more adaptable and versatile assembling climate. Laborers can zero in on errands that require imagination, critical thinking, and direction, while robots handle normal, redundant, or unsafe assignments. This cooperative collaboration upgrades in general functional adaptability and responsiveness to changing business sector requests.

Difficulties and Contemplations:

Be that as it may, the joining of mechanical technology and savvy plant innovations isn't without challenges. The underlying interest in these advances can be critical, presenting monetary hindrances for certain makers. Furthermore, the requirement for gifted faculty to work, program, and keep up with these high level frameworks features the significance of progressing labor force improvement and preparing drives.

The security of interconnected frameworks in brilliant production lines is likewise a basic thought. With expanded network comes the gamble of digital dangers and assaults on touchy assembling information. Hearty network safety measures are crucial for shield against expected disturbances and breaks.

2.9 Supply Chain Optimization

Production network streamlining has turned into a basic concentration for organizations trying to upgrade proficiency, diminish costs, and work on generally functional execution. In the powerful worldwide commercial center, where supply chains can be complicated and complex, upgrading the progression of merchandise, data, and funds is fundamental for keeping an upper hand.

Start to finish Perceivability:

One vital part of store network improvement is accomplishing start to finish perceivability. This includes ongoing checking and following of products as they travel through the inventory network. Cutting edge innovations, for example, IoT gadgets, RFID labels, and GPS following, give granular bits of knowledge into the area, condition, and status of items. This perceivability empowers organizations to recognize bottlenecks, smooth out processes, and proactively address likely disturbances.

Information Driven Direction:

Information is at the core of production network enhancement. The assortment and examination of immense measures of information permit organizations to go with informed choices that drive productivity and responsiveness. Progressed investigation, AI, and computerized reasoning empower prescient displaying, anticipating request, and advancing stock levels. This information driven approach limits vulnerabilities, improves estimating precision, and works with proactive dynamic across the whole production network.

Stock Administration and Request Determining:

Successful stock administration is a foundation of production network streamlining. Adjusting stock levels to satisfy client need while limiting overabundance stock is a sensitive however essential undertaking. By utilizing information examination and AI calculations, organizations can acquire experiences into request examples, irregularity, and market patterns. This empowers them to advance stock levels, decrease conveying costs, and guarantee ideal accessibility of items.

Cooperative Production network Organizations:

Cooperation among inventory network accomplices is one more key component of advancement. Laying areas of strength for out and joint effort channels with providers, makers, wholesalers, and retailers encourages a more responsive and nimble inventory network. Shared information and ongoing data trade empower all accomplices to adjust their exercises, synchronize processes, and all in all answer changes popular or production network disturbances.

Innovation Incorporation:

The coordination of trend setting innovations is instrumental in accomplishing store network enhancement. Computerization, advanced mechanics, and man-made reasoning smooth out routine errands, diminish mistakes, and upgrade by and large functional effectiveness. Stockroom computerization, for example, further develops request satisfaction processes, lessens lead times, and limits manual dealing with. The consistent mix of innovations across the store network environment guarantees a more firm and synchronized activity.

Strength and Hazard Moderation:

Store network streamlining implies building versatility and alleviating chances. This incorporates recognizing expected chances, whether they be international, ecological, or functional, and carrying out techniques to oversee and alleviate these dangers. Organizations are progressively embracing risk the board structures and possibility wanting to guarantee congruity notwithstanding unexpected disturbances.

2.10 Agriculture and Food Production

Farming and food creation stand at the convergence of mechanical development, supportability, and worldwide interest. The reception of cutting edge innovations in agribusiness has changed customary cultivating works on, upgrading effectiveness, diminishing ecological effect, and guaranteeing food security.

Accuracy agribusiness, empowered by advancements like GPS, sensors, and robots, permits ranchers to improve asset use. These devices give continuous information on soil conditions, crop wellbeing, and weather conditions, empowering exact dynamic in regions like water system, treatment, and bug control. This increments yields as well as limits asset wastage and ecological effect.

The incorporation of Web of Things (IoT) gadgets further adds to savvy cultivating rehearses. Associated sensors in the field accumulate information on temperature, mugginess, and yield development, making a complete comprehension of the rural biological system. This information driven approach empowers ranchers to screen and oversee crops from a distance, working on functional productivity and diminishing the requirement for manual mediation.

Biotechnology assumes a significant part in present day farming, offering hereditarily changed crops with upgraded protection from vermin, illnesses, and ecological stressors. Hereditary designing can possibly address worldwide difficulties, for example, environmental change and populace development, by creating crops that flourish in assorted conditions and offer higher healthful benefit.

Maintainability has turned into a point of convergence in farming, determined to offset food creation with ecological stewardship. Agro-ecological rehearses advance biodiversity, soil wellbeing, and regular vermin control, adding to versatile and supportable cultivating frameworks. Natural cultivating, regenerative horticulture, and agroforestry are building up some decent momentum as ranchers and purchasers focus on harmless to the ecosystem and socially capable food creation.

As the worldwide populace keeps on developing, the test of guaranteeing food security turns out to be really squeezing. Innovation driven developments in horticulture support efficiency as well as assume a crucial part in tending to the intricacies of taking care of a developing populace. By embracing feasible works on, utilizing information examination, and tackling biotechnological progressions, farming and food creation are ready to satisfy the needs representing things to come while limiting their environmental impression.

2.11 Precision Farming

Accuracy cultivating, frequently alluded to as accuracy horticulture, addresses a groundbreaking way to deal with crop the board that use innovation to enhance different parts of cultivating rehearses. At its center, accuracy cultivating plans to upgrade effectiveness, decrease asset information sources, and increment by and large efficiency by using constant information and cutting edge innovations.

The execution of Worldwide Situating Framework (GPS) innovation is a foundation of accuracy cultivating. GPS empowers ranchers to exactly guide and screen their fields, considering precise route of farming hardware and designated utilization of assets. This degree of accuracy in field activities limits covers, decreases squander, and streamlines the utilization of data sources like manures and pesticides.

Sensors and information examination are vital parts of accuracy cultivating, furnishing ranchers with important experiences into soil conditions, crop wellbeing, and natural elements. Soil sensors measure dampness levels and supplement content, permitting ranchers to fit water system and treatment practices to the particular requirements of every region inside a field. Remote detecting advances, including satellite and robot symbolism, give high-goal information on crop development, empowering early location of potential issues like illnesses or vermin invasions.

Variable rate innovation (VRT) is one more key element of accuracy cultivating. This innovation permits ranchers to shift the pace of data sources in view of the particular necessities of various regions inside a field. By progressively changing cultivating rates, compost application, and water system levels, ranchers can advance asset usage and upgrade by and large yield execution.

Accuracy cultivating contributes not exclusively to further developed asset productivity yet additionally to manageability. By limiting the natural effect of horticultural practices, accuracy cultivating lines up with the objectives of manageable agribusiness. The reception of accuracy cultivating methods holds the possibility to address worldwide difficulties, including food security and ecological manageability, as ranchers endeavor to create more with less assets in a quickly impacting world.

2.12 Crop Monitoring

Crop observing is a urgent part of present day farming, working with information driven independent direction and upgrading by and large harvest the board rehearses. Progresses in innovation, especially in the domains of remote detecting and information examination, have altered the manner in which ranchers screen and evaluate the wellbeing and development of their harvests.

Remote detecting innovations, like satellite symbolism and robots, give ranchers a far reaching and constant perspective on their fields. These devices catch itemized data about crop wellbeing, development designs, and ecological circumstances. Satellite symbolism, with its worldwide inclusion, empowers huge scope observing, while drones offer high-goal information at an additional restricted and granular level. This abundance of data engages ranchers to distinguish potential issues almost immediately, including vermin pervasions, infections, or supplement lacks.

The coordination of multispectral and hyperspectral imaging further upgrades crop observing abilities. These advancements consider the examination of explicit frequencies of light reflected by crops, giving bits of knowledge into their physiological circumstances. Ranchers can recognize pressure factors, evaluate chlorophyll levels, and settle on informed conclusions about water system, treatment, and bug control.

Information examination assumes an essential part in making an interpretation of crude data into significant experiences. By handling and deciphering the tremendous measures of information produced through crop checking, ranchers can make nitty gritty guides of their fields, outlining regions that might require explicit mediations. This accuracy takes into account focused on and productive asset allotment, upgrading the utilization of contributions while limiting waste.

Crop observing not just adds to expanded yields and asset productivity yet additionally lines up with reasonable cultivating rehearses. By taking on information driven approaches, ranchers can go with informed choices that advance natural stewardship, diminish the environmental impression of agribusiness, and add to the general strength of the cultivating biological system. As innovation keeps on propelling, crop checking will stay a foundation of current horticulture, engaging ranchers to explore the intricacies of harvest the executives in a consistently changing rural scene.

3

Chapter 3

Transforming the Workplace: AI and Employment

The combination of Computerized reasoning (artificial intelligence) into the work environment is changing the business scene in significant ways, reshaping position jobs, processes, and the actual idea of work itself. As artificial intelligence innovations keep on propelling, their effect on business traverses different enterprises, going from assembling and money to medical care and client support. Understanding the multilayered ramifications of simulated intelligence on business is urgent for people, organizations, and policymakers as they explore the advancing scene of the cutting edge work environment.

Man-made intelligence and Occupation Mechanization:

One of the most noticeable parts of computer based intelligence's effect on work is its job in work robotization. Man-made intelligence driven mechanization includes the utilization of shrewd machines to perform undertakings generally completed by people.

Standard and redundant errands, especially those including information investigation, can be executed all the more proficiently by computer based intelligence calculations, prompting the robotization of specific work capabilities. While this upgrades efficiency and smoothes out processes, it raises worries about work relocation and the requirement for reskilling the labor force to adjust to the changing requests of the gig market.

Work Dislodging and Reskilling:

The feeling of dread toward work dislodging because of computerization has been a subject of conversation and concern. As simulated intelligence assumes control over routine undertakings, some work jobs might become out of date, affecting specific areas and occupations. Nonetheless, history has shown that innovative progressions frequently set out new open doors and occupation classifications. The vital lies in reskilling and upskilling the labor force to line up with the advancing requests of the computerized economy. Instructive foundations, organizations, and states assume a vital part in working with progressing learning and improvement to guarantee that specialists are furnished with the abilities required for arising jobs in the artificial intelligence driven working environment.

Man-made intelligence as an Efficiency Sponsor:

In opposition to the apprehension about broad employment cutback, man-made intelligence can possibly go about as an efficiency supporter, enlarging human capacities instead of supplanting them completely. In numerous businesses, computer based intelligence is conveyed to deal with routine and tedious undertakings, permitting human specialists to zero in on more complicated, imaginative, and vital parts of their jobs. This cooperative connection among people and simulated intelligence upgrades generally speaking efficiency and can prompt the formation of new, seriously satisfying open positions that influence the remarkable qualities of both.

Improving Inventiveness and Advancement:

Artificial intelligence's effect on business reaches out past robotization to encouraging inventiveness and advancement. Artificial intelligence calculations can dissect tremendous datasets, distinguish designs, and create experiences that might escape human examination alone. In imaginative fields like plan, advertising, and content creation, simulated intelligence devices aid ideation, content streamlining, and customized client encounters. This cooperative methodology among man-made intelligence and human imagination opens new roads for development, pushing the limits of what can be accomplished in different enterprises.

Simulated intelligence in Client assistance and Collaboration:

The combination of simulated intelligence in client care is an outstanding illustration of how innovation is reshaping the idea of business. Chatbots, remote helpers, and computer based intelligence driven specialized instruments are progressively dealing with routine client requests, giving moment reactions, and smoothing out assistance processes.

While this further develops effectiveness and responsiveness, it additionally accentuates the significance of human touchpoints in client co-operations. Human specialists assume a vital part in resolving complex issues, feeling for clients, and guaranteeing a customized and nuanced administration experience.

The Ascent of Remote Work and Joint effort:

Computer based intelligence's impact on business is interwoven with the changing elements of the work environment, especially the ascent of remote work and virtual coordinated effort. Simulated intelligence driven devices work with consistent correspondence, project the board, and joint effort across geologically scattered groups. AI calculations examine work examples, inclinations, and information to improve work processes, empowering groups to work all the more productively no matter what their actual area. The union of man-made intelligence and remote work mirrors an essential change in how work is coordinated and executed, underscoring adaptability and versatility in the computerized age.

Computer based intelligence in Medical services:

In the medical services area, simulated intelligence is upsetting diagnostics, therapy arranging, and patient consideration. Clinical experts influence man-made intelligence calculations to break down clinical pictures, recognize oddities, and help with diagnosing sicknesses. While man-made intelligence upgrades the precision and speed of diagnostics, it doesn't supplant the skill and sympathy of medical care experts. All things considered, it permits medical services laborers to zero in on customized patient consideration, therapy techniques, and complex clinical navigation, stressing a cooperative model among simulated intelligence and human skill.

Computer based intelligence in Assembling and Industry 4.0:

The assembling area has gone through a huge change with the coming of simulated intelligence and Industry 4.0. Shrewd manufacturing plants influence artificial intelligence driven computerization, mechanical technology, and IoT advancements to improve creation processes, upgrade quality control, and limit free time. While these advances add to expanded productivity and accuracy, human laborers stay fundamental for errands that require imagination, critical thinking, and navigation. The coordination of computer based intelligence in assembling features the potential for human-machine cooperation to make more versatile and responsive creation environments.

Computer based intelligence and Moral Contemplations:

As computer based intelligence turns out to be profoundly implanted in the work environment, moral contemplations become principal. Issues connected with predisposition in man-made intelligence calculations, straightforwardness in direction, and the capable utilization of computer based intelligence advances require cautious consideration.

Guaranteeing decency and value in man-made intelligence applications, moderating potentially negative side-effects, and laying out clear moral rules are fundamental for cultivating a working environment climate that focuses on both development and moral contemplations.

The Fate of Work:

The eventual fate of work in the time of simulated intelligence is dynamic and developing. While specific routine undertakings might be computerized, the interest for abilities like decisive reasoning, the capacity to understand anyone on a deeper level, and versatility turns out to be more articulated. The positions representing things to come are probably going to include a crossover model where people team up with savvy machines to use the qualities of both. Persistent learning, versatility, and a proactive way to deal with embracing innovative progressions will be critical for people exploring the changing scene of work.

3.1 Job Displacement vs. Job Creation

The powerful exchange between work dislodging and work creation is a focal subject in the continuous development of the work market, and the coming of mechanical progressions, especially Man-made brainpower (computer based intelligence), has brought this polarity into sharp concentration. The groundbreaking effect of simulated intelligence on work is mind boggling, set apart by the synchronous uprooting of specific positions and the making of new open doors that line up with the advancing requirements of the computerized economy. Understanding this equilibrium is critical for people, organizations, and policymakers as they explore the many-sided scene of labor force elements.

Work Removal:

The reconciliation of man-made intelligence and computerization into different businesses has prompted worries about the removal of specific work jobs. Standard and tedious assignments, especially those including information examination and manual cycles, are defenseless to robotization. In areas, for example, fabricating, routine mechanical production system occupations are progressively being taken care of by automated frameworks, prompting a change in the ranges of abilities requested by the gig market. Additionally, in authoritative jobs, simulated intelligence fueled devices are robotizing assignments like information passage, archive handling, and fundamental client assistance.

The apprehension about work dislodging isn't unwarranted, and verifiable points of reference, like the Modern Upheaval, have demonstrated the way that innovative progressions can prompt the outdated nature of specific occupations.

Be that as it may, the extraordinary idea of innovation likewise achieves a rebuilding of occupation jobs as opposed to a discount disposal. While routine errands might be computerized, the accentuation movements to jobs that require innovativeness, decisive reasoning, critical thinking, and the ability to understand people on a profound level — credits that are innately human and less inclined to computerization.

Reskilling and Upskilling:

Relieving the effect of occupation relocation includes a purposeful exertion towards reskilling and upskilling the labor force. The fast advancement of innovation expects people to adjust and get new abilities that are sought after in the computerized economy. Instructive foundations, organizations, and states assume a critical part in working with continuous learning chances to furnish laborers with the abilities required for arising jobs.

Reskilling includes gaining new abilities pertinent to a changing position market, while upskilling includes upgrading existing abilities to fulfill the needs of further developed or concentrated jobs. Drives, for example, online courses, professional preparation projects, and organizations between instructive establishments and businesses add to making a labor force that is lithe and strong even with mechanical interruptions.

Arising Position Jobs:

The other side of occupation dislodging is the development of new position jobs that are made as an immediate consequence of innovative headways. The ascent of man-made intelligence has prompted the production of jobs, for example, information researchers, AI engineers, simulated intelligence trained professionals, and computerization specialists. These positions require a profound comprehension of artificial intelligence advancements, programming dialects, and the capacity to break down and decipher information — a range of abilities that was not as pervasive in customary work jobs.

Besides, as enterprises take on computer based intelligence for different applications, there is a rising interest for people who can create, execute, and keep up with these artificial intelligence frameworks. Moral contemplations connected with computer based intelligence, like predisposition alleviation and straightforwardness, have led to jobs zeroed in on artificial intelligence morals and administration. The interdisciplinary idea of man-made intelligence additionally sets out open doors for people with foundations in fields like brain research, social science, and morals to add to the capable turn of events and arrangement of artificial intelligence advances.

Man-made intelligence Expanded Jobs:

One more component of the gig market change is the idea of man-made intelligence expanded jobs, where astute machines team up with human laborers to improve efficiency and independent direction. Instead of supplanting people, computer based intelligence is frequently coordinated into work jobs to deal with routine and information concentrated errands, permitting human laborers to zero in on mind boggling, imaginative, and vital parts of their work.

In medical care, for instance, simulated intelligence is utilized to dissect clinical pictures and aid diagnostics, empowering medical care experts to pursue more educated choices. In client support, chatbots handle routine requests, opening up human specialists to address more perplexing and nuanced client issues. This cooperative methodology highlights the potential for computer based intelligence to expand human capacities and make a more productive and powerful labor force.

Business venture and Development:

The appearance of artificial intelligence additionally energizes business venture and advancement, prompting the making of new companies and private ventures that influence artificial intelligence innovations. Business people are investigating novel utilizations of man-made intelligence in different ventures, from medical services and money to horticulture and training. This flood in enterprising action sets out new position open doors inside new businesses as well as adds to the more extensive financial biological system.

Business people and private ventures assume a critical part in driving development and adjusting to the changing mechanical scene. As they investigate computer based intelligence driven arrangements and plans of action, they produce interest for specific abilities and skill. This request stretches out past specialized jobs to envelop regions like showcasing, deals, and client service, making an expanding influence of occupation creation in different areas.

The Gig Economy and Adaptable Work:

The development of the gig market is likewise apparent in the ascent of the gig economy and adaptable work game plans. Innovation stages that interface specialists, self employed entities, and temporary laborers with bosses have acquired unmistakable quality. Man-made intelligence driven stages coordinate people with explicit abilities to present moment or undertaking based open doors, giving adaptability and independence in work plans.

While the gig economy presents difficulties connected with employer stability, it likewise offers people the capacity to broaden their abilities, work on numerous undertakings at the same time, and make an arrangement of encounters. This shift towards adaptable work lines up with the powerful idea of the advanced economy, where people might take part in numerous jobs or activities all through their vocations.

The Job of Strategy and Administration:

Exploring the fragile harmony between work uprooting and creation requires smart approach and administration measures. Policymakers assume a basic part in molding the administrative structure, guaranteeing that specialists are secured, and organizations stick to moral and dependable man-made intelligence rehearses. Strategies that advance re-skilling drives, support long lasting learning, and encourage coordinated effort between instructive organizations and ventures are fundamental parts of a proactive way to deal with labor force change.

Legislatures can likewise boost organizations to put resources into preparing programs, support innovative work in arising advances, and establish a climate helpful for development and business. Moral rules for artificial intelligence advancement and organization, combined with straightforward revealing systems, add to building trust in simulated intelligence advancements and alleviating potential dangers related with work removal.

Comprehensive and Impartial Methodologies:

A comprehensive and impartial methodology is essential to guaranteeing that the advantages of mechanical headways are shared across assorted fragments of the populace. Abberations in admittance to schooling, preparing potential open doors, and business assets can compound existing disparities. Endeavors to address these differences through designated drives, grants, and local area based programs add to making a more impartial labor force.

Moreover, cultivating variety in the turn of events and organization of computer based intelligence advancements is fundamental for forestalling predispositions and guaranteeing that computer based intelligence frameworks are planned considering a great many points of view. Comprehensive practices in the working environment add to a more imaginative and versatile labor force that can successfully explore the intricacies of the developing position market.

3.2 Reskilling and Upskilling the Workforce

The quick progression of innovation, especially in fields like Manmade reasoning (computer based intelligence) and mechanization, is reshaping the business scene at an extraordinary speed. As specific work jobs become robotized and new ones arise, reskilling and upskilling have become basic for people and associations the same. The continuous course of gaining new abilities and improving existing ones isn't just a reaction to the developing requests of the gig market yet additionally a proactive methodology to guarantee labor force dexterity, development, and seriousness in the computerized age.

The Requirement for Reskilling and Upskilling:

The basic for reskilling and upskilling originates from the groundbreaking effect of innovation on the idea of work.

Robotization and computer based intelligence innovations are progressively dealing with standard and dreary errands, delivering specific work jobs old. Thus, laborers need to adjust to the changing requests of their enterprises by obtaining new abilities that line up with arising advancements and occupation prerequisites. Reskilling includes mastering completely new abilities pertinent to an alternate work or industry, while upskilling centers around upgrading existing abilities to satisfy the needs of further developed or concentrated jobs.

The requirement for reskilling and upskilling reaches out across different areas, from assembling and money to medical services and data innovation. For instance, as customary assembling jobs become mechanized, laborers might have to reskill to work and keep up with the canny machines that have assumed control over routine errands. In the monetary area, the ascent of FinTech expects workers to upskill in information examination, network safety, and advanced finance. In medical services, experts might have to reskill to comprehend and use simulated intelligence devices for diagnostics and therapy arranging.

The Job of Deep rooted Learning:

The idea of deep rooted learning lies at the center of reskilling and upskilling. Before, schooling was many times seen as a limited period of life, with people procuring abilities during their initial years and depending on those abilities all through their vocations. Nonetheless, the fast speed of innovative change has delivered this conventional model old. Long lasting mastering perceives that ceaseless expertise obtaining is fundamental for people to stay pertinent and versatile despite advancing advancements and occupation prerequisites.

Long lasting learning can take different structures, including formal instruction, online courses, studios, accreditations, and hands on preparing. Instructive establishments, businesses, and people themselves all assume significant parts in encouraging a culture of persistent learning. Perceiving the benefit of continuous schooling is fundamental for people to remain cutthroat in the gig market and for associations to keep a gifted and imaginative labor force.

Industry Coordinated effort and Associations:

Reskilling and upskilling drives are best when there is coordinated effort between instructive foundations and enterprises. Industry pioneers can give bits of knowledge into the particular abilities and mastery they expect in their labor force. This cooperation guarantees that instructive projects are lined up with the functional requirements of the gig market, lessening the abilities hole and improving the employability of people.

Organizations among organizations and instructive foundations can take different structures, including entry level positions, apprenticeships, and joint preparation programs.

These organizations work with a consistent progress for people from figuring out how to pragmatic application, guaranteeing that they get hypothetical information as well as active involvement with true settings. Industry joint effort additionally empowers instructive foundations to likewise keep up to date with the most recent mechanical turns of events and designer their projects.

Mechanical Learning Stages:

The advanced age has introduced a period where learning isn't bound to conventional study halls. Innovative learning stages, frequently open on the web, have democratized instruction and made reskilling and upskilling more available than any time in recent memory. Stages like Coursera, edX, LinkedIn Learning, and Udacity offer a different scope of courses, confirmations, and degree programs covering different fields and ranges of abilities.

These stages give adaptability, permitting people to learn at their own speed and on their own timetable. Whether it's securing coding abilities, learning information examination, or dominating task the board, these stages offer a huge range of assets for people hoping to upgrade their ranges of abilities. The gamification of realizing, where progress is followed and accomplishments are perceived, adds a connecting with component that persuades students to continue in their instructive excursions.

Government Drives and Arrangements:

Legislatures assume an essential part in encouraging a culture of reskilling and upskilling. Perceiving the more extensive cultural advantages of a gifted and versatile labor force, numerous states have acquainted drives and strategies with help progressing learning. This incorporates monetary impetuses, tax cuts, and awards to urge people and organizations to put resources into schooling and preparing.

Government-supported projects may likewise zero in on tending to explicit abilities holes in key ventures. For instance, on the off chance that there is a deficiency of network safety experts, the public authority might carry out drives to boost people to reskill or upskill in this field. By adjusting strategies to the developing requirements of the gig market, legislatures can add to a stronger and cutthroat labor force.

Delicate Abilities and The capacity to understand people on a deeper level:

While specialized abilities are imperative in the advanced age, the significance of delicate abilities and the capacity to appreciate anyone on a deeper level couldn't possibly be more significant. As mechanization assumes control over routine errands, human abilities like correspondence, joint effort, flexibility, and compassion become progressively significant. Reskilling and upskilling endeavors ought not be restricted to specialized capability however ought to likewise incorporate the improvement of these fundamental relational and profound abilities.

The capacity to work really in groups, convey thoughts obviously, and explore complex social elements is significant in the advanced working environment. The capacity to understand individuals at their core, which incorporates mindfulness, self-guideline, social mindfulness, and relationship the executives, upgrades initiative characteristics and cultivates a positive and cooperative workplace. Reskilling and upskilling programs that integrate these delicate abilities add to the all encompassing improvement of people, making them balanced and versatile experts.

Difficulties and Obstructions:

In spite of the reasonable advantages of reskilling and upskilling, there are difficulties and boundaries that people and associations might experience. One significant test is the view of an absence of time, especially for people who are now working all day. Adjusting work, family, and instructive responsibilities can overwhelm. Adaptable learning choices and business upheld preparing during work hours can assist with beating this test.

Monetary limitations may likewise represent an obstruction, particularly for people who may not manage the cost of conventional instructive projects. Government endowments, grants, and boss supported preparing projects can lighten these monetary weights. Moreover, there might be a protection from change, both with respect to people and associations. A mentality that values constant learning and embraces flexibility is fundamental for defeating this obstruction.

Future Patterns in Reskilling and Upskilling:

As innovation keeps on developing, a few patterns are probably going to shape the scene of reskilling and upskilling later on. Customized learning pathways, empowered by computer based intelligence and AI calculations, will turn out to be more common. These pathways will be custom fitted to individual learning styles, inclinations, and vocation objectives, giving a more effective and customized instructive experience.

Microcredentials and computerized identifications, which offer a more granular and explicit acknowledgment of abilities, will acquire conspicuousness. These certifications, frequently procured through short courses or centered preparing programs, give an unmistakable and irrefutable way for people to exhibit their mastery in unambiguous regions. Businesses, thus, can utilize these microcredentials as important signs of a competitor's abilities and capacities.

The idea of ceaseless evaluation and input will become indispensable to reskilling and upskilling drives. Instead of depending entirely on conventional tests, constant assessment strategies, including project-based evaluations and certifiable reenactments, will give a more complete comprehension of a singular's abilities and preparation for explicit jobs.

3.3 AI and Human Collaboration

The reconciliation of Man-made reasoning (computer based intelligence) into different aspects of our lives affects human business, dynamic cycles, and by and large cultural designs. One vital part of this convergence among computer based intelligence and human undertakings is the cooperation between wise machines and individuals. Rather than a situation where computer based intelligence replaces human jobs completely, the common pattern is toward a cooperative relationship, where man-made intelligence increases human capacities, prompting upgraded efficiency, development, and critical thinking across different spaces.

Increased Knowledge:

The idea of increased knowledge typifies that simulated intelligence frameworks are planned not to supplant human insight yet to supplement and upgrade it. In contrast to full robotization, where machines work autonomously, expanded knowledge centers around utilizing simulated intelligence to enable human navigation. In this cooperative model, artificial intelligence frameworks dissect huge datasets, distinguish examples, and proposition experiences, giving people important data to go with additional educated choices.

Expanded insight is especially clear in information serious fields like medical care, money, and examination. In medical care, man-made intelligence helps clinical experts by dissecting clinical pictures, distinguishing peculiarities, and recommending expected analyze. In finance, simulated intelligence calculations dissect market patterns and information, offering experiences that illuminate human dealers' choices. This cooperative methodology improves productivity by joining the insightful ability of artificial intelligence with the nuanced understanding and inventiveness of human specialists.

Mental Cooperation:

Mental cooperation alludes to the mix of computer based intelligence innovations into cooperative devices and stages, encouraging more viable correspondence and navigation inside groups. These instruments use normal language handling, AI, and prescient examination to upgrade joint effort via robotizing routine undertakings, blending data, and giving setting mindful ideas.

In the work environment, mental joint effort devices are changing the way that groups work. Chatbots and remote helpers work with constant correspondence, plan gatherings, and recover data, smoothing out managerial errands. Progressed examination implanted in coordinated effort stages offer information driven experiences, assisting groups with settling on better-informed choices. The cooperative energy among artificial intelligence and human coordinated effort improves efficiency and inventiveness, permitting people to zero in on errands that require decisive reasoning, the ability to appreciate anyone on a deeper level, and complex critical thinking.

Computer based intelligence in Imaginative Businesses:

In opposition to worries about artificial intelligence supplanting human imagination, there is a developing acknowledgment that computer based intelligence can be a strong colleague in imaginative businesses. Man-made intelligence apparatuses are currently utilized in music piece, workmanship age, and content creation. For instance, computer based intelligence calculations can examine immense datasets of music to produce structures that resound with explicit classifications or styles. In visual expressions, computer based intelligence fueled calculations help craftsmen by producing clever thoughts, recommending plan components, or in any event, making visual substance in view of explicit rules.

The cooperation among computer based intelligence and human imagination extends the potential outcomes in imaginative fields, testing ordinary thoughts of origin and pushing the limits of creative articulation. It features the potential for artificial intelligence to go about as an impetus for development, offering new points of view and supporting imaginative experts in their undertakings.

Human-Driven simulated intelligence Plan:

The joint effort among computer based intelligence and people requires a human-driven plan approach, underlining moral contemplations, straightforwardness, and client experience. As artificial intelligence frameworks become more coordinated into day to day existence, planning frameworks that line up with human qualities and needs is fundamental. Moral man-made intelligence standards, like reasonableness, responsibility, and straightforwardness, guide the improvement of frameworks that focus on human prosperity and limit expected inclinations.

Client experience (UX) plan assumes a urgent part in guaranteeing that man-made intelligence connection points are natural, easy to understand, and open. Cooperative apparatuses and stages that consistently incorporate man-made intelligence ought to upgrade, as opposed to prevent, the client experience. This accentuation on human-driven plan encourages trust and acknowledgment of simulated intelligence advancements, working with their viable mix into different parts of human existence.

Simulated intelligence in Customized Help:

Customized simulated intelligence associates epitomize the cooperative potential among people and insightful machines. These collaborators, like Siri, Google Colleague, and Amazon's Alexa, use normal language handling and AI to figure out client inclinations, expect needs, and execute assignments. From setting suggestions to giving weather conditions refreshes, these artificial intelligence partners consistently coordinate into everyday schedules, expanding human capacities in data recovery and undertaking robotization.

In addition, in the domain of medical services, man-made intelligence controlled remote helpers can give customized wellbeing bits of knowledge, medicine updates, and, surprisingly, consistent reassurance. These applications feature the potential for simulated intelligence to improve the personal satisfaction by offering custom-made help and backing, taking special care of individual necessities and inclinations.

Simulated intelligence in Schooling:

In the field of schooling, simulated intelligence fills in as a cooperative device that upholds the two teachers and understudies. Computer based intelligence controlled versatile learning stages examine individual understudy execution, distinguish solid areas and shortcoming, and designer instructive substance to meet explicit advancing necessities. This customized approach improves the opportunity for growth, permitting understudies to advance at their own speed and get designated help.

Instructive simulated intelligence apparatuses additionally help educators via computerizing authoritative assignments, giving information driven experiences into understudy execution, and offering assets for illustration arranging. The cooperative utilization of simulated intelligence in schooling expects to make a more comprehensive and viable learning climate, utilizing innovation to address individual learning styles and encourage a more profound comprehension of topic.

Difficulties and Contemplations:

In spite of the various advantages of man-made intelligence human cooperation, challenges and moral contemplations persevere. Work uprooting concerns are in many cases raised, especially in ventures where robotization is pervasive. The trepidation that simulated intelligence might supplant specific work jobs is legitimate, requiring a proactive way to deal with reskilling and upskilling the labor force to adjust to the changing requests of the gig market.

Moral contemplations connected with predisposition in man-made intelligence calculations additionally present difficulties. Assuming that computer based intelligence frameworks are prepared on one-sided datasets, they might propagate and try and worsen existing social predispositions. Addressing these predispositions requires a coordinated work to guarantee decency, straightforwardness, and responsibility in computer based intelligence plan and sending.

Protection concerns emerge as man-made intelligence frameworks gather and dissect immense measures of individual information to offer customized types of assistance. Finding some kind of harmony between customized help and it is pivotal to protect individual security. Laying out powerful information assurance measures, client assent components, and straightforward information utilization approaches is crucial for assemble and keep up with trust in simulated intelligence frameworks.

The Eventual fate of man-made intelligence Human Joint effort:

The direction of simulated intelligence human coordinated effort highlights an inexorably interwoven relationship, where clever machines act as significant teammates, not substitutions. Future advancements are probably going to zero in on refining simulated intelligence capacities to more readily grasp human setting, feelings, and goals, working with additional regular and natural collaborations. Progressions in normal language handling, the capacity to appreciate anyone on a profound level acknowledgment, and context oriented understanding will add to the consistent joining of man-made intelligence into different parts of human existence.

As computer based intelligence advances develop, the accentuation will move toward interdisciplinary coordinated effort, uniting specialists from different fields to use the qualities of both man-made intelligence and human mastery. Moral structures and administrative guidelines will keep on creating, directing the dependable and evenhanded arrangement of simulated intelligence frameworks.

4

Chapter 4

Ethical Considerations in AI Development

The fast progression of Man-made brainpower (man-made intelligence) innovations has introduced another period of potential outcomes and difficulties, inciting a basic assessment of the moral contemplations encompassing artificial intelligence improvement. As canny machines become progressively coordinated into different features of society, moral worries emerge connected with predisposition, straightforwardness, responsibility, protection, and the more extensive cultural effect of computer based intelligence frameworks. Addressing these moral contemplations is essential to guaranteeing the dependable and valuable arrangement of artificial intelligence advancements.

Inclination and Reasonableness:

One of the premier moral worries in artificial intelligence improvement is the potential for predisposition in calculations.

Artificial intelligence frameworks are prepared on huge datasets, and if these datasets contain intrinsic predispositions, the computer based intelligence models can sustain and try and enhance those inclinations in their dynamic cycles. Predispositions can arise in different structures, including racial, orientation, financial, and social inclinations, mirroring the verifiable and cultural setting of the information.

Guaranteeing decency in artificial intelligence frameworks requires a proactive methodology all through the improvement lifecycle. This remembers careful assessment and relief of predispositions for preparing information, straightforward divulgence of likely predispositions in man-made intelligence applications, and continuous observing and assessment to address any unseen side-effects. Analysts and designers are progressively zeroing in on creating strategies to distinguish and correct predispositions in computer based intelligence calculations, stressing the requirement for decency and value in simulated intelligence frameworks.

Straightforwardness and Logic:

The misty idea of some simulated intelligence calculations presents difficulties to understanding how choices are made, especially in complex frameworks like profound brain organizations. Absence of straightforwardness and reasonableness can sabotage client trust and raise moral worries, particularly in applications where choices influence people's lives, like in medical care, money, and law enforcement.

Finding some kind of harmony between the intricacy of cutting edge simulated intelligence models and the requirement for straightforwardness is a basic moral thought. Endeavors are in progress to foster logical man-made intelligence (XAI) strategies that give experiences into how man-made intelligence frameworks show up at explicit choices. By improving straightforwardness, clients can all the more likely comprehend and trust man-made intelligence frameworks, encouraging responsibility and working with moral navigation.

Responsibility and Obligation:

As simulated intelligence innovations become more inescapable, characterizing and designating responsibility for the activities of clever machines turns into a complex moral test. Inquiries concerning who is liable for the results of man-made intelligence choices, particularly in instances of mischief or unseen side-effects, feature the requirement for clear systems for responsibility.

The obligation regarding computer based intelligence frameworks reaches out across the whole improvement lifecycle, including scientists, designers, policymakers, and end-clients. Moral contemplations direct that those engaged with simulated intelligence improvement ought to be responsible for the moral ramifications of their work.

Laying out rules and principles for moral simulated intelligence improvement, alongside legitimate structures that characteristic obligation, is fundamental to guarantee responsibility and alleviate expected adverse consequences.

Protection Concerns:

Computer based intelligence frameworks frequently expect admittance to a lot of information to learn and make forecasts. The assortment, stockpiling, and usage of individual information raise critical protection concerns. Safeguarding people's security is a major moral thought in artificial intelligence improvement, especially in applications like medical care, money, and observation.

Carrying out hearty security measures, like information anonymization, encryption, and adherence to protection guidelines, is crucial for address these worries. Finding some kind of harmony between the requirement for information driven experiences and shielding individual protection requires cautious thought and the joining of security improving innovations into simulated intelligence frameworks.

Security and Vigor:

The moral ramifications of simulated intelligence stretch out to contemplations of safety and strength. Simulated intelligence frameworks can be powerless against antagonistic assaults, where purposefully controlled input information prompts wrong or destructive results. Guaranteeing the security and vigor of simulated intelligence models is vital to forestall malevolent double-dealing and unseen side-effects.

Tending to security concerns includes executing thorough testing, approval, and checking processes during the improvement of man-made intelligence frameworks. Moral contemplations direct that designers focus on the strength of simulated intelligence models to antagonistic endeavors and persistently update guards against arising dangers.

Cultural Effect and Inclusivity:

Artificial intelligence innovations can have far reaching cultural effects, impacting business, availability, and financial elements. The moral obligation in simulated intelligence improvement reaches out to surveying and relieving expected unfortunate results on networks and people. Guaranteeing that the advantages of man-made intelligence are conveyed impartially and don't worsen existing disparities is a critical moral thought.

Advancing inclusivity includes effectively tending to predispositions in man-made intelligence frameworks, taking into account the assorted requirements of various client gatherings, and staying away from the making of advancements that may excessively affect underestimated networks. Drawing in with partners, including agents from impacted networks, in the plan and organization of simulated intelligence frameworks is fundamental for encourage inclusivity and address expected cultural irregular characteristics.

Natural Effect:

The ecological effect of computer based intelligence framework, especially enormous scope AI models, is arising as a moral thought. Preparing modern simulated intelligence models requires significant computational power, prompting huge energy utilization. Moral computer based intelligence advancement ought to consider the ecological results of asset concentrated preparing processes.

Endeavors to address the natural effect of artificial intelligence incorporate examination into energy-productive calculations, manageable figuring rehearses, and the investigation of elective techniques for model preparation. Moral contemplations in man-made intelligence advancement stretch out past the quick cultural effect on envelop more extensive biological ramifications, lining up with feasible and naturally dependable practices.

Cooperation and Worldwide Administration:

Man-made intelligence advancement frequently rises above public boundaries, bringing up issues about the requirement for worldwide norms, coordinated effort, and administration. Moral contemplations include laying out systems for worldwide collaboration to address shared difficulties, including information assurance, algorithmic responsibility, and the mindful organization of artificial intelligence advances.

Cooperative endeavors between legislatures, industry partners, and worldwide associations are fundamental to lay out moral standards and rules that guide the turn of events and organization of man-made intelligence innovations on a worldwide scale. Moral contemplations in this setting include advancing straightforwardness, forestalling the abuse of man-made intelligence for pernicious purposes, and encouraging a co-operative way to deal with tending to the complex moral difficulties that man-made intelligence presents.

Continuous Moral Reflection:

The field of man-made intelligence is dynamic and ceaselessly developing, requiring progressing moral reflection and transformation to new difficulties. Moral contemplations ought to be an indispensable piece of the improvement interaction, including interdisciplinary joint effort, progressing exchange, and responsiveness to arising moral worries.

Moral survey sheets, interdisciplinary councils, and industry principles associations assume essential parts in encouraging a culture of moral computer based intelligence improvement. Drawing in with different viewpoints, including ethicists, social researchers, and delegates from impacted networks, adds to a thorough comprehension of the moral ramifications of man-made intelligence innovations.

4.1 Bias and Fairness in AI

Predisposition and reasonableness in Man-made brainpower (man-made intelligence) frameworks have become essential moral worries as these advancements pervade different parts of our lives. Computer based intelligence, especially AI models, depends vigorously on information for preparing, and assuming this information reflects authentic inclinations, the subsequent models can propagate and try and compound those predispositions. Understanding and alleviating predisposition in computer based intelligence is fundamental to guarantee evenhanded and fair results in dynamic cycles. This investigation digs into the intricacies of predisposition and reasonableness in artificial intelligence, looking at the main drivers, outcomes, and continuous endeavors to address these moral difficulties.

The Idea of Predisposition in simulated intelligence:

Predisposition in simulated intelligence alludes to the presence of precise and unreasonable partiality or segregation towards specific people or gatherings. This predisposition can appear in different structures, including racial inclination, orientation inclination, financial inclination, and social predisposition. The hidden issue frequently emerges from the information used to prepare simulated intelligence models, which might reflect verifiable disparities and biases.

Preparing information can encode cultural inclinations since it frequently reflects human choices and activities. For example, in the event that verifiable employing rehearses were one-sided against specific segment gatherings, an artificial intelligence model prepared on this information could accidentally propagate those predispositions while making recruiting suggestions. Essentially, one-sided policing might bring about man-made intelligence frameworks that excessively target explicit networks.

Understanding the wellsprings of predisposition in artificial intelligence is a complex test. Predispositions can be presented during information assortment, preprocessing, include choice, and model preparation. Absence of variety in the groups creating artificial intelligence frameworks can likewise add to one-sided results. The intricacy of these issues requires a far reaching and interdisciplinary way to deal with recognize, measure, and address inclinations really.

Results of Predisposition in artificial intelligence:

The results of predisposition in artificial intelligence can be extensive and influence people and networks in different ways. In regions like money, work, law enforcement, and medical services, one-sided simulated intelligence calculations can sustain and enhance existing social imbalances.

In recruiting and business, one-sided calculations may accidentally lean toward specific segment bunches over others, supporting existing abberations in the labor force. In law enforcement, one-sided calculations utilized for risk appraisal may lopsidedly mark people from underestimated networks as higher gamble, prompting vile sentences and propagating fundamental imbalances.

In addition, one-sided medical care calculations can prompt abberations in therapy proposals, analysis, and admittance to clinical assets. Assuming that an artificial intelligence framework is prepared dominatingly on information from explicit segment gatherings, it may not sum up well to different populaces, coming about in poor medical care results for specific networks.

Tending to Predisposition and Guaranteeing Reasonableness:

Endeavors to address predisposition in computer based intelligence and advance reasonableness are picking up speed across the scholarly world, industry, and policymaking. These endeavors incorporate a scope of procedures, from further developing information assortment practices to growing more comprehensive and delegate calculations.

Different and Agent Information:

Guaranteeing that preparing information is different and delegate of the populace is an essential move toward moderating predisposition. This includes gathering information from many sources and guaranteeing that it incorporates adequate models from underrepresented gatherings. Nonetheless, accomplishing wonderful portrayal can be testing, and progressing endeavors are important to persistently refine and increase datasets.

Algorithmic Straightforwardness:

Straightforwardness in simulated intelligence calculations is significant for understanding their dynamic cycles. By making calculations more interpretable, designers and clients can distinguish and address inclinations really. Reasonable artificial intelligence (XAI) strategies mean to give experiences into how artificial intelligence frameworks show up at explicit choices, working with straightforwardness and responsibility.

Reasonableness Mindful Models:

Scientists are effectively chipping away at creating decency mindful AI models. These models are intended to expressly represent reasonableness limitations during preparing, keeping the calculation from learning or supporting one-sided designs. Decency mindful models frequently include integrating reasonableness measurements and imperatives straightforwardly into the enhancement cycle.

Moral Rules and Principles:

The turn of events and adherence to moral rules and principles assume a vital part in advancing reasonableness in man-made intelligence. Industry associations, research foundations, and states arc chipping away at laying out systems that frame moral standards for man-made intelligence advancement and sending. These rules underline reasonableness, straightforwardness, responsibility, and inclusivity.

Predisposition Identification and Reviewing:

Consistently reviewing and assessing man-made intelligence frameworks for predisposition is fundamental. Different apparatuses and methods have been created to identify and evaluate predispositions in calculations. Predisposition recognition includes examining the model's result across various segment gatherings to distinguish and redress inconsistencies. Continuous checking guarantees that any arising predispositions are tended to immediately.

Various Advancement Groups:

A different and comprehensive group of designers, information researchers, and specialists can add to all the more morally sound computer based intelligence frameworks. Different groups bring a scope of points of view and encounters, assisting with distinguishing and relieve predispositions that may be disregarded in homogenous groups. Inclusivity in computer based intelligence improvement is critical for building frameworks that function admirably for all clients.

Difficulties and Constraints:

In spite of continuous endeavors to address predisposition in artificial intelligence, a few difficulties and limits endure. Accomplishing ideal reasonableness in simulated intelligence frameworks is a subtle objective because of the inborn intricacy of cultural predispositions and the trouble of foreseeing every single imaginable outcome. Furthermore, compromises might emerge between various reasonableness measurements, requiring cautious thought of the moral ramifications of explicit decisions.

One more test lies in offsetting reasonableness with execution. Making progress toward decency shouldn't think twice about exactness and adequacy of simulated intelligence models. Accomplishing an equilibrium that ideally addresses both decency and execution stays a continuous test, requiring nonstop refinement and assessment of calculations.

Additionally, predispositions can advance after some time, and artificial intelligence frameworks might battle to adjust to changing accepted practices and elements. This powerful nature of predispositions requires an adaptable and versatile way to deal with inclination moderation, guaranteeing that simulated intelligence frameworks stay lined up with developing moral principles.

The Job of Schooling and Mindfulness:

Schooling and mindfulness are imperative parts in the more extensive work to address predisposition and reasonableness in man-made intelligence. Expanding mindfulness about the potential predispositions intrinsic in simulated intelligence frameworks and the moral contemplations encompassing their improvement is fundamental for the two designers and end-clients. Instructive drives can enable people to basically assess simulated intelligence advancements, pose appropriate inquiries about their decency, and backer for mindful simulated intelligence rehearses.

Tending to predisposition in artificial intelligence likewise includes furnishing engineers with the information and apparatuses important to perceive and relieve predispositions all through the improvement lifecycle. Proceeded with instruction and preparing programs that underscore moral computer based intelligence rehearses, social capability, and the social ramifications of innovation add to building a more educated and faithful artificial intelligence local area.

Future Headings and Moral Contemplations:

As artificial intelligence advances keep on developing, moral contemplations around inclination and decency will stay at the very front of conversations. Future bearings include refining existing systems, growing new procedures for inclination alleviation, and ceaselessly adjusting to arising difficulties. The moral scene of man-made intelligence will require continuous interdisciplinary joint effort, including ethicists, social researchers, technologists, and policymakers.

Moreover, moral contemplations reach out past specialized perspectives to include more extensive cultural ramifications. The moral obligation of simulated intelligence designers incorporates effectively captivating with impacted networks, looking for input according to different viewpoints, and integrating criticism into the advancement cycle. Fabricating morally sound simulated intelligence frameworks requires a pledge to straightforwardness, responsibility, and inclusivity at each progressive phase.

4.2 Privacy Concerns and Data Security

Protection concerns and information security have arisen as basic contemplations in the time of fast mechanical headway, especially with the expansion of Computerized reasoning (artificial intelligence) and information driven advancements. As people and associations produce, offer, and store huge measures of individual data, the need to defend protection and guarantee strong information safety efforts has become foremost. This investigation dives into the complexities of security concerns and information security, analyzing the difficulties, results, and advancing procedures to safeguard delicate data in the computerized age.

Protection Worries in the Computerized Scene:

The computerized scene has changed how individual data is gathered, handled, and used, leading to a bunch of security concerns. Online exercises, virtual entertainment collaborations, internet business exchanges, and the utilization of shrewd gadgets add to the age of broad information profiles for people. The assortment of such information, frequently without unequivocal client assent or information, raises worries about the disintegration of individual protection.

One of the essential security concerns spins around the commodification of individual information. Organizations, sponsors, and information handles frequently influence client data to convey designated ads, customized administrations, and proposals. While customization can upgrade client encounters, it additionally brings up issues about the moral utilization of individual information and the potential for manipulative practices.

Additionally, the rising predominance of reconnaissance advancements, both by states and confidential substances, has led to worries about meddlesome checking and the potential for misuse. Observation cameras, facial acknowledgment frameworks, and other checking apparatuses can catch people's exercises without their mindfulness, prompting banters about the harmony between open wellbeing and individual security.

Information Security Difficulties:

Guaranteeing information security is fundamental for defend individual data from unapproved access, breaks, and noxious exercises. The difficulties in keeping up with hearty information security are different and consistently developing, mirroring the refinement of digital dangers. A few key difficulties include:

Digital Assaults and Breaks:

Cybercriminals utilize various strategies, including hacking, phishing, and malware assaults, to acquire unapproved admittance to delicate information. Information breaks can have serious outcomes, prompting fraud, monetary misfortunes, and reputational harm for people and associations the same.

Insider Dangers:

Insiders, like workers or workers for hire with admittance to delicate data, represent a critical danger to information security. Whether accidental or malignant, insider activities can bring about information releases, unapproved divulgences, or other security episodes.

Insufficient Safety efforts:

Inadequate safety efforts, like frail passwords, absence of encryption, and obsolete programming, make weaknesses that can be taken advantage of by cybercriminals. Associations should constantly refresh and improve their security conventions to address arising dangers.

Information Block attempt and Snoopping:

The capture of information during transmission, known as information block attempt or snoopping, is a worry, particularly in unstable organizations. Without encryption and secure correspondence conventions, delicate data can be caught, prompting possible breaks.

Outsider Dangers:

Teaming up with outsider specialist co-ops, sellers, or accomplices presents extra dangers. In the event that these elements don't focus on strong information security rehearses, they may coincidentally uncover delicate data, affecting the essential association and its clients.

Outcomes of Protection Breaks and Insufficient Information Security:

Protection breaks and lacking information safety efforts can have extreme ramifications for people, associations, and society at large. A portion of the eminent repercussions include:

Wholesale fraud:

Taken individual data, like names, addresses, and monetary subtleties, can be taken advantage of for wholesale fraud. Cybercriminals might utilize this data to open fake records, make unapproved buys, or take part in other crimes, hurting the impacted people.

Monetary Misfortunes:

Breaks that compromise monetary information, for example, charge card data or ledger subtleties, can bring about monetary misfortunes for the two people and associations. Recuperating from such misfortunes can be tedious and testing.

Reputational Harm:

Information breaks frequently lead to reputational harm for associations, dissolving trust among clients, clients, and accomplices. Reestablishing trust after a security occurrence can be an extensive and complex cycle, influencing the drawn out reasonability of the impacted element.

Lawful and Administrative Outcomes:

Security breaks can prompt legitimate repercussions, particularly in districts with rigid information assurance regulations. Associations might confront fines, lawful activities, and administrative investigation assuming they neglect to carry out satisfactory information safety efforts or disregard protection guidelines.

Social Designing and Control:

Uncovered individual data can be utilized for social designing assaults, where cybercriminals control people by utilizing their own information against them. This can incorporate designated phishing endeavors, tricks, or different types of control.

Loss of Protection and Independence:

Protection breaks add to the disintegration of people's security and independence. The information that individual data isn't secure can prompt a feeling of weakness and hesitance to take part in web-based exercises.

Advancing Techniques for Information Security and Security Insurance:

Tending to protection concerns and upgrading information security requires a multi-layered and versatile methodology. A few procedures are being utilized to moderate dangers and safeguard delicate data:

Encryption:

Encryption is a key device for safeguarding information both on the way and very still. Encoding delicate data guarantees that regardless of whether unapproved access happens, the information stays mixed up without the suitable unscrambling keys.

Multifaceted Validation (MFA):

Executing MFA adds an extra layer of safety by expecting clients to give different types of distinguishing proof prior to accessing frameworks or records. This decreases the gamble of unapproved access, regardless of whether login accreditations are compromised.

Customary Reviews and Evaluations:

Directing standard security reviews and evaluations recognizes weaknesses and shortcomings in existing frameworks. Proactive measures, for example, infiltration testing, can uncover potential passage focuses for digital assailants.

Client Instruction and Mindfulness:

Teaching clients about security best practices, the dangers of phishing, and the significance of solid passwords adds to a greater security-cognizant climate. Informed clients are more averse to succumb to social designing strategies.

Information Minimization and Maintenance Approaches:

Embracing information minimization rehearses includes gathering and holding just the fundamental data. Furthermore, carrying out information maintenance strategies guarantees that data isn't put away endlessly, diminishing the likely effect of an information break.

Secure Advancement Practices:

Incorporating security into the advancement lifecycle is essential. Sticking to get coding works on, leading code surveys, and executing security conventions during the advancement stage lessen the probability of weaknesses.

Outsider Security Evaluations:

Directing security evaluations of outsider sellers and specialist organizations recognizes potential dangers related with outer coordinated efforts. Guaranteeing that outsiders stick to hearty security norms is fundamental for in general information security.

Protection by Plan:

Consolidating protection contemplations all along, known as security by configuration, includes coordinating security highlights into the improvement cycle. This approach underlines building frameworks that focus on client security and information assurance.

Consistence with Information Insurance Guidelines:

Complying with information security guidelines, like the Overall Information Assurance Guideline (GDPR) or the Medical coverage Compactness and Responsibility Act (HIPAA), guarantees that associations meet lawful necessities connected with information security and protection.

Occurrence Reaction Plans:

Creating and consistently refreshing occurrence reaction plans empowers associations to answer successfully to security episodes. Having a clear cut plan limits the effect of a break and works with an ideal and facilitated reaction.

The Eventual fate of Information Security and Protection:

As innovation keeps on propelling, the fate of information security and protection will be formed by progressing advancement, developing dangers, and the improvement of new defensive measures. A few vital contemplations for the future include:

Man-made intelligence Controlled Security Arrangements:

The combination of simulated intelligence in security arrangements holds guarantee for further developed danger discovery and moderation. Computer based intelligence can examine designs, recognize abnormalities, and answer security episodes progressively, upgrading in general information security.

Blockchain Innovation:

Blockchain, with its decentralized and alter safe nature, is being investigated as a way to upgrade information security. Executing blockchain in specific applications can give a straightforward and secure method for overseeing and check information exchanges.

Protection Upgrading Advances:

Protection upgrading advances, like differential security and homomorphic encryption, are acquiring consideration. These advancements plan to safeguard delicate data while as yet taking into consideration significant examination and information usage.

Global Cooperation:

Digital dangers frequently rise above public lines, requiring global joint effort on network protection drives. Cooperative endeavors can prompt the advancement of worldwide guidelines, data sharing, and facilitated reactions to digital dangers.

Lawful and Moral Systems:

The foundation and refinement of lawful and moral systems will keep on assuming an essential part. Legislatures, administrative bodies, and industry affiliations will cooperate to make and refresh guidelines that address arising difficulties in information security and protection.

Strengthening of People:

Engaging people to have more prominent command over their own information is a developing pattern. Advances, for example, decentralized character arrangements and individual information vaults plan to give people more independence and assent over how their data is utilized.

4.3 Accountability and Transparency

Responsibility and straightforwardness are primary standards in the moral turn of events and sending of advances, especially with regards to Man-made brainpower (man-made intelligence). As man-made intelligence frameworks become progressively coordinated into different features of society, holding engineers, associations, and leaders responsible for their manifestations is significant. This investigation digs into the interconnected ideas of responsibility and straightforwardness in artificial intelligence, analyzing their importance, challenges, and the developing procedures to guarantee mindful man-made intelligence rehearses.

Responsibility in artificial intelligence:

Responsibility in artificial intelligence alludes to the obligation of people, associations, and substances engaged with the turn of events, organization, and utilization of computer based intelligence frameworks. It envelops the commitment to guarantee that computer based intelligence advancements are morally planned, stick to legitimate norms, and think about the possible cultural effects of their execution. The complex idea of responsibility includes different partners, including designers, policymakers, administrative bodies, and end-clients.

Designer Responsibility:

Engineers assume a critical part in the responsibility of simulated intelligence frameworks. Their obligation reaches out to planning calculations that are fair, unprejudiced, and straightforward. Recognizing the expected results of man-made intelligence choices and effectively attempting to alleviate inclinations and accidental results are fundamental parts of engineer responsibility.

Hierarchical Responsibility:

Associations conveying artificial intelligence frameworks bear responsibility for the advances they bring into the market. This incorporates guaranteeing that man-made intelligence applications line up with moral standards, lawful prerequisites, and industry principles. Laying out inside rules, leading effect evaluations, and cultivating a culture of liability add to hierarchical responsibility.

Client Responsibility:

End-clients of simulated intelligence frameworks likewise bear a degree of responsibility. Understanding the constraints and expected predispositions of computer based intelligence advances is critical for going with informed choices. Clients ought to effectively participate in the capable utilization of artificial intelligence, addressing results that appear to be unreasonable or one-sided and giving criticism to further develop framework execution.

Administrative and Strategy Responsibility:

Administrative bodies and policymakers assume a basic part in considering the computer based intelligence biological system responsible. Laying out clear rules, guidelines, and lawful systems guarantees that man-made intelligence advances comply with moral standards and don't encroach on individual privileges. Policymakers are responsible for establishing a climate that encourages advancement while defending the public interest.

Moral Audit Sheets:

Moral audit sheets or councils can give an extra layer of responsibility. These interdisciplinary bodies evaluate the moral ramifications of artificial intelligence projects, investigate likely inclinations, and guarantee that innovative work line up with moral rules. Moral survey processes add to the capable direct of artificial intelligence research.

Challenges in Guaranteeing Responsibility:

While the idea of responsibility is principal, carrying out compelling systems for responsibility in man-made intelligence presents difficulties:

Intricacy and Haziness:

The intricacy of man-made intelligence calculations, especially in profound learning and brain organizations, can make it trying to follow and comprehend the dynamic cycle. The obscurity of specific models prevents the capacity to distinguish and correct predispositions, bringing up issues about responsibility.

Absence of Guideline and Norms:

The shortfall of far reaching guidelines and extensive principles presents difficulties in considering designers and associations responsible. The quickly advancing nature of computer based intelligence innovation frequently outperforms the improvement of administrative structures, making holes in responsibility.

Worldwide Nature of computer based intelligence:

Man-made intelligence improvement frequently happens on a worldwide scale, rising above public limits. Organizing global endeavors for responsibility becomes complicated, requiring joint effort between assorted lawful, social, and administrative settings.

Potentially negative results:

In spite of engineers' earnest attempts, artificial intelligence frameworks might deliver potentially negative results. Considering people responsible for these results, particularly in situations where the results are hard to anticipate, presents difficulties in deciding the degree of obligation.

Dynamic Nature of man-made intelligence:

The dynamic and versatile nature of artificial intelligence frameworks presents difficulties in keeping up with responsibility after some time. As artificial intelligence advancements develop and gain from new information, their way of behaving may change, requiring continuous investigation and updates to responsibility measures.

Straightforwardness in man-made intelligence:

Straightforwardness in man-made intelligence includes going with the choice making cycles of simulated intelligence frameworks reasonable and interpretable to important partners, including engineers, clients, and impacted networks. Straightforward man-made intelligence frameworks are those where the thinking behind choices is clear, permitting clients to understand how and why a specific result is reached.

Reasonableness and Interpretability:

Reasonableness alludes to the capacity to explain how a simulated intelligence framework shows up at a particular choice. Interpretability, then again, includes figuring out the more extensive working of the framework. The two viewpoints add to straightforwardness by demystifying the frequently complicated and murky nature of artificial intelligence calculations.

Easy to use Points of interaction:

Making easy to understand interfaces that impart man-made intelligence choices in a fathomable way improves straightforwardness. Giving clients experiences into what calculations work and the variables meaning for their choices cultivates trust and engages clients to pursue informed decisions.

Interdisciplinary Joint effort:

Accomplishing straightforwardness frequently requires interdisciplinary joint effort between man-made intelligence designers, area specialists, ethicists, and ease of use subject matter experts. Cooperative endeavors guarantee that the plan and correspondence of man-made intelligence frameworks consider assorted viewpoints, making them more straightforward and justifiable.

Clear Documentation:

Archiving the advancement interaction, information sources, and algorithmic decisions adds to straightforwardness. Clear documentation permits outer commentators, moral audit sheets, and clients to evaluate the decency and unwavering quality of man-made intelligence frameworks.

Open Source and Open Information Practices:

Embracing open source and open information practices can upgrade straightforwardness in man-made intelligence improvement. Making source code and datasets openly available works with outside investigation, empowers joint effort, and empowers a more exhaustive comprehension of simulated intelligence frameworks.

Challenges in Guaranteeing Straightforwardness:
Discovery Models:

Some artificial intelligence models, especially complex brain organizations, work as secret elements, meaning their interior operations are trying to decipher. Accomplishing straightforwardness in such models is troublesome, prompting worries about responsibility and likely predispositions.

Compromises Among Precision and Reasonableness:

There can be compromises between the precision of computer based intelligence models and their reasonableness. More perplexing models frequently accomplish higher precision however may forfeit straightforwardness. Finding some kind of harmony between these elements stays a test in computer based intelligence improvement.

Delicate Data and Protection:

Straightforward man-made intelligence frameworks may coincidentally uncover delicate data, prompting protection concerns. Finding some kind of harmony among straightforwardness and the insurance of individual information is significant for moral simulated intelligence rehearses.

Social and Logical Varieties:

Straightforwardness necessities might fluctuate across social and relevant settings. What is viewed as straightforward and reasonable in one setting may not be all around appropriate, requiring nuanced ways to deal with straightforwardness.

Instructive Holes:

Clients, policymakers, and, surprisingly, a few designers might come up short on vital comprehension of man-made intelligence innovations to decipher and request straightforwardness. Tending to instructive holes is fundamental for encouraging a culture of straightforwardness and responsibility.

Advancing Procedures for Responsibility and Straightforwardness:

Interdisciplinary Coordinated effort:

Empowering interdisciplinary cooperation includes uniting specialists from different fields, including man-made intelligence improvement, morals, humanism, and regulation. This approach guarantees that different viewpoints add to the moral and straightforward improvement of artificial intelligence frameworks.

Moral Audit Cycles:

Executing moral audit processes, like institutional survey sheets in research, can upgrade responsibility. These audit sheets evaluate the moral ramifications of computer based intelligence projects, investigate possible inclinations, and guarantee that examination lines up with moral rules.

Advancement of Moral Rules:

The plan and adherence to moral rules add to responsibility and straightforwardness. Industry associations, research organizations, and legislatures can foster clear moral structures that guide man-made intelligence advancement and sending.

Public Commitment and Discussion:

Drawing in the general population in conversations about simulated intelligence advancements guarantees that a wide range of viewpoints is thought of. Public counsels can give significant experiences into the cultural effect of computer based intelligence frameworks and add to responsible direction.

Regulation and Guideline:

States and administrative bodies can assume a urgent part in guaranteeing responsibility and straightforwardness through regulation and guideline. Laying out clear rules and legitimate structures considers people and associations responsible for the moral turn of events and organization of man-made intelligence.

Algorithmic Effect Evaluations:

Directing algorithmic effect appraisals includes assessing the expected social, monetary, and moral ramifications of artificial intelligence frameworks before their arrangement. This proactive methodology recognizes and address expected inclinations and issues connected with responsibility.

Ceaseless Checking and Examining:

Executing consistent observing and reviewing of artificial intelligence frameworks post-arrangement is fundamental. This continuous examination guarantees that the framework's conduct stays in accordance with moral norms and considers opportune mediation in the event of issues.

Chapter 5

The Impact on Society: Challenges and Opportunities

The combination of Computerized reasoning (simulated intelligence) into different parts of society delivers a range of difficulties and valuable open doors that shape the manner in which we live, work, and connect. As man-made intelligence innovations advance, their effect on society turns out to be progressively articulated, impacting different areas like instruction, medical care, business, and administration. This investigation dives into the complex ramifications of simulated intelligence on society, tending to both the difficulties that need cautious route and the potential open doors that emerge for positive change.

Difficulties of man-made intelligence In the public arena:

Work Dislodging:

One of the essential difficulties presented by man-made intelligence is the potential for work relocation.

Computerization and man-made intelligence driven innovations have the ability to play out specific errands more productively than people, prompting worries about the effect on work across different enterprises. Occupations that include normal, monotonous errands are especially helpless to computerization.

Moral Contemplations:

Moral worries in computer based intelligence envelop issues connected with predisposition, security, responsibility, and the possible abuse of cutting edge innovations. The inborn predispositions present in preparing information can bring about unfair results, presenting difficulties in accomplishing decency and value. Furthermore, worries about the dependable utilization of man-made intelligence in reconnaissance, navigation, and different applications require cautious thought.

Security Disintegration:

The broad assortment and investigation of information by man-made intelligence frameworks raise security concerns. As man-made intelligence calculations process immense measures of individual data to go with forecasts and choices, there is a gamble of unapproved access, information breaks, and the expected abuse of delicate information. Finding some kind of harmony between utilizing information for development and safeguarding individual security is a mind boggling challenge.

Absence of Straightforwardness:

The absence of straightforwardness in artificial intelligence calculations presents difficulties in understanding how choices are made. Complex brain organizations and AI models frequently work as secret elements, making it hard for people to appreciate the thinking behind simulated intelligence created results. This haziness can add to question and frustrate the acknowledgment of man-made intelligence advances.

Algorithmic Inclination and Reasonableness:

Algorithmic predisposition is an unavoidable test in man-made intelligence, mirroring the predispositions present in the information utilized for preparing. Assuming verifiable information contains prejudicial examples, computer based intelligence models might sustain and try and intensify these predispositions. Accomplishing reasonableness in computer based intelligence direction is a continuous test that requires persistent endeavors to distinguish, moderate, and forestall one-sided results.

Advanced Gap:

The reception and openness of man-made intelligence innovations add to the computerized partition, making differences among people and networks with admittance to cutting edge innovations and those without. Addressing this gap is critical to guarantee that the advantages of artificial intelligence are comprehensive and don't intensify existing social imbalances.

Security Dangers:

Simulated intelligence frameworks can be defenseless against security chances, including ill-disposed assaults and abuse of weaknesses. The rising refinement of digital dangers presents difficulties in shielding simulated intelligence frameworks against vindictive exercises. Guaranteeing strong network safety measures is

fundamental to forestall unapproved access, information control, and other security breaks.

Reliance on simulated intelligence Frameworks:

Society's rising dependence on artificial intelligence frameworks raises worries about reliance and the expected outcomes of framework disappointments. In basic areas like medical services, money, and transportation, the glitch or abuse of simulated intelligence advances can have serious repercussions. Laying out emergency courses of action and safeguard instruments is significant to relieve these dangers.

Influence on Emotional well-being:

The fast speed of mechanical progressions, including man-made intelligence driven mechanization, can add to work related pressure, vulnerability, and changes in the idea of work. These elements, joined with the potential for work dislodging, may have suggestions for psychological well-being and prosperity, expecting thoughtfulness regarding the cultural effect of computer based intelligence on the labor force.

Chances of man-made intelligence In the public arena:

Upgraded Proficiency and Efficiency:

Man-made intelligence advances can possibly fundamentally upgrade effectiveness and efficiency across different areas. Robotization of routine errands permits people to zero in on more perplexing, imaginative, and esteem added exercises. In ventures like assembling, coordinated factors, and client care, artificial intelligence driven robotization can prompt smoothed out activities and expanded yield.

Progressions in Medical services:

Computer based intelligence presents extraordinary open doors in medical services, going from diagnostics and therapy wanting to tranquilize disclosure and customized medication. AI calculations can dissect clinical information, recognize examples, and help medical services experts in pursuing more precise and opportune choices. This can possibly work on quiet results, diminish expenses, and advance clinical exploration.

Training and Customized Learning:

Artificial intelligence in schooling offers amazing open doors for customized growth opportunities. Versatile learning stages can fit instructive substance to individual understudy needs, working with a more compelling and drawing in educational experience. Artificial intelligence driven instructive apparatuses additionally can possibly give important experiences into understudy execution and assist instructors with improving educating techniques.

Advancement and Innovativeness:

Man-made intelligence advances add to development and innovativeness across different businesses. In fields like plan, workmanship, and content creation, artificial intelligence apparatuses can help and expand human capacities. For instance, generative computer based intelligence models can be utilized to make workmanship, music, and writing, cultivating new types of imaginative articulation.

Further developed Direction:

Simulated intelligence frameworks, outfitted with cutting edge examination and prescient abilities, can aid information driven navigation. In business, money, and administration, simulated intelligence driven experiences empower more educated and key direction. These advancements can possibly streamline asset allotment, improve risk the executives, and add to more powerful strategy arranging.

Propels in Logical Exploration:

Man-made intelligence speeds up logical exploration by examining huge datasets, recreating complex situations, and distinguishing designs that might escape human specialists. In fields like stargazing, genomics, and materials science, simulated intelligence driven apparatuses add to leap forwards and disclosures that can possibly address squeezing world-wide difficulties.

Human-man-made intelligence Cooperation:

The cooperative energy among people and man-made intelligence advances can prompt strong joint effort. In areas like client assistance, man-made intelligence fueled chatbots can deal with routine requests, opening up human specialists to zero in on additional mind boggling associations. Human-artificial intelligence joint effort can possibly intensify human abilities and make more compelling and effective work processes.

Ecological Maintainability:

Man-made intelligence innovations add to ecological supportability endeavors through applications, for example, energy improvement, environment displaying, and normal asset the board. Simulated intelligence driven arrangements can help screen and relieve natural difficulties, giving bits of knowledge to additional reasonable practices and direction.

5.1 Socioeconomic Implications

The reconciliation of Man-made reasoning (computer based intelligence) into different features of society delivers significant financial ramifications that shape the elements of work, business, and more extensive monetary designs. As artificial intelligence innovations advance, their effect on the financial scene turns out to be progressively apparent, introducing the two difficulties and open doors. This investigation dives into the multi-layered ramifications of man-made intelligence on financial designs, resolving issues, for example, business designs, pay disparity, and the change of enterprises.

1. **Work Examples and Occupation Relocation:**
   One of the main financial ramifications of artificial intelligence is the change of business designs. Computer based intelligence driven robotization can possibly smooth out and improve routine errands across different businesses, prompting changes in the idea of work. While simulated intelligence can set out new position open doors, it additionally raises worries about work uprooting, especially in jobs that include redundant and routine assignments. Enterprises like assembling, coordinated factors, and client assistance are seeing the effect of computer based intelligence driven mechanization on customary work jobs.
   The shift towards mechanization can bring about a polarization of the gig market, with a developing interest for profoundly gifted, innovation situated jobs and a decrease in specific daily schedule, manual positions. This pattern adds to an abilities hole, requiring endeavors in reskilling and upskilling the labor force to adjust to the developing requests of the gig market. Policymakers and organizations need to team up to formulate techniques that address these movements, guaranteeing that the advantages of computer based intelligence driven efficiency are shared across a different scope of laborers.

2. **Pay Imbalance and Abilities Variations:**
   The financial effect of man-made intelligence stretches out to pay imbalance and abilities incongruities. As man-made intelligence advances become essential to ventures, people with the abilities to create, execute, and oversee computer based intelligence frameworks are popular, prompting wage differentials among gifted and untalented laborers. This abilities based pay hole can fuel existing financial abberations.
   Tending to these difficulties requires a deliberate exertion in

giving admittance to schooling and preparing programs that outfit people with the abilities essential for the simulated intelligence driven labor force. Drives zeroed in on shutting the abilities hole, particularly in innovation related fields, can add to a more comprehensive financial scene.

In addition, arrangements that advance deep rooted acquiring and ceaseless expertise improvement are fundamental for relieving the adverse consequences of pay disparity coming about because of man-made intelligence reception.

3. **Business and Monetary Advancement:**
Simulated intelligence likewise presents valuable open doors for business venture and financial advancement. The availability of man-made intelligence apparatuses and innovations empowers little and medium-sized ventures (SMEs) to use progressed investigation, computerization, and information driven experiences. This democratization of innovation can cultivate monetary development and advancement, permitting organizations to contend all the more really in the computerized economy.

Business visionaries can outfit artificial intelligence for item advancement, market investigation, and client commitment, making new plans of action and upsetting customary ventures. Policymakers can uphold this pattern by establishing an empowering climate for new companies and SMEs to get to artificial intelligence assets, financing, and mentorship. The cultivating of advancement biological systems that support coordinated effort between business people, scientists, and financial backers can add to monetary dynamism and occupation creation.

4. **Change of Ventures and Financial Areas:**
Computer based intelligence is catalyzing the change of ventures, prompting changes in financial areas and worth chains. Enterprises like medical care, money, assembling, and farming are encountering the incorporation of simulated intelligence driven arrangements that enhance processes, further develop

proficiency, and drive advancement. This change has suggestions for labor force creation, work jobs, and the general construction of ventures.

In medical care, for instance, simulated intelligence applications range from analytic apparatuses to customized medication, improving patient consideration and therapy results. In finance, man-made intelligence driven calculations are utilized for risk appraisal, extortion identification, and portfolio the board. The computerization of assembling processes through artificial intelligence controlled advanced mechanics is reshaping the creation scene. While these progressions bring proficiency gains, they likewise require changes in labor force abilities and an essential way to deal with dealing with the cultural effect of industry changes.

5. **Remote Work and Computerized Incorporation:**
   Computer based intelligence innovations, combined with progressions in correspondence and network, have worked with the ascent of remote work. The Coronavirus pandemic sped up this pattern, with associations embracing artificial intelligence driven coordinated effort apparatuses, menial helpers, and remote checking frameworks. While remote work offers adaptability and valuable open doors for computerized consideration, it likewise raises worries about admittance to innovation, the advanced separation, and variations in remote work capacities.

   Guaranteeing advanced consideration includes tending to framework holes, giving admittance to reasonable and dependable web availability, and outfitting people with the computerized abilities important for remote work. Policymakers can assume a part in encouraging computerized consideration drives that overcome any barrier among metropolitan and country regions, guaranteeing that the advantages of man-made intelligence driven remote work are open to a different and geologically scattered labor force.

6. **Social Effect and Local area Elements:**
   The financial effect of man-made intelligence reaches out past

monetary elements to impact social elements and local area structures. The progressions in business designs, abilities prerequisites, and industry changes can reshape local area characters and modify customary models of work and social collaboration. As man-made intelligence advancements reclassify the idea of occupations, networks might encounter shifts in socioeconomics, relocation examples, and local area union.

Guaranteeing positive social effect requires proactive measures that address possible disturbances to networks. This remembers ventures for local area based schooling and preparing programs, drives that help neighborhood organizations in embracing artificial intelligence advancements, and approaches that consider the social ramifications of simulated intelligence driven changes in business. Local area commitment and coordinated effort between neighborhood partners, organizations, and policymakers are fundamental for cultivating strength and versatility even with financial changes.

7. **Moral Contemplations and Social Obligation:**
The inescapable reception of artificial intelligence raises moral contemplations that have social and financial ramifications. Issues, for example, algorithmic predisposition, protection concerns, and the dependable utilization of computer based intelligence in dynamic cycles require cautious consideration. Guaranteeing that artificial intelligence advancements stick to moral standards is fundamental for building trust in their cultural effect.

Organizations and associations sending computer based intelligence frameworks bear a social obligation to focus on moral contemplations in artificial intelligence improvement and sending. This includes straightforwardness in calculations, decency in dynamic cycles, and dynamic endeavors to alleviate predispositions. Furthermore, policymakers assume a part in laying out moral rules and guidelines that guide the dependable utilization of computer based intelligence advances, defending people and networks from likely mischief.

8. **Strategy Systems for Financial Effect:**

The complex financial ramifications of simulated intelligence require thorough strategy systems that address the diverse difficulties and open doors. Policymakers assume a vital part in molding the direction of man-made intelligence reception, guaranteeing that its advantages are circulated evenhandedly and potential unfortunate results are relieved.

Key components of successful arrangement structures include:

Schooling and Preparing Projects:

Executing drives that emphasis on schooling and preparing projects to furnish people with the abilities required in the computer based intelligence driven labor force. This incorporates coordinated efforts between instructive establishments, organizations, and government offices to make pertinent and available learning open doors.

Work Market Strategies:

Creating adaptable work market strategies that help the change of laborers in businesses impacted by man-made intelligence driven mechanization. This includes retraining and reskilling programs, joblessness backing, and approaches that energize labor force flexibility.

Advanced Consideration Drives:

Putting resources into computerized consideration drives to connect the advanced gap and guarantee that the advantages of man-made intelligence innovations, including remote work open doors, are open to a different populace. This incorporates framework improvement, reasonable web access, and advanced education programs.

Development Biological systems:

Encouraging advancement environments that help business, new companies, and SMEs in utilizing simulated intelligence innovations. This includes establishing a climate that energizes coordinated effort between industry, the scholarly community, and examination foundations, working with the interpretation of investigation into viable applications.

Moral Rules and Guidelines:

Laying out clear moral rules and guidelines that administer the turn of events and sending of computer based intelligence advancements. This incorporates resolving issues of algorithmic predisposition, security assurance, and responsibility in computer based intelligence frameworks. Policymakers assume a significant part in making an administrative structure that guarantees the dependable utilization of simulated intelligence.

Local area Commitment and Social Effect Appraisals:

Empowering people group commitment in the turn of events and execution of computer based intelligence advances. Social effect appraisals can assist with recognizing expected difficulties and open doors intended for networks, educating the plan regarding arrangements and mediations that alleviate unfortunate results and upgrade positive results.

Worldwide Cooperation:

Advancing global coordinated effort and data sharing on accepted procedures, guidelines, and approaches connected with artificial intelligence. Given the worldwide idea of computer based intelligence improvement and sending, coordinated effort between nations can add to a fit methodology that tends to financial difficulties on a more extensive scale.

5.2 Education and AI Literacy

The convergence of training and Computerized reasoning (manmade intelligence) has introduced an extraordinary time, forming the manner in which understudies learn, instructors instruct, and schooling systems work. The joining of simulated intelligence in training holds the commitment of customized opportunities for growth, worked on instructive results, and upgraded managerial productivity. Nonetheless, it additionally raises significant contemplations connected with morals, security, and the requirement for far reaching simulated intelligence education. This investigation digs into the advancing scene of schooling and man-made intelligence, analyzing the open doors, challenges, and the basic of cultivating artificial intelligence proficiency in instructive settings.

1. **Open doors in Training and man-made intelligence:**
   The coordination of artificial intelligence in schooling delivers a heap of chances to upgrade the growth opportunity for under-studies, enable teachers, and improve regulatory cycles.

Customized Learning:

Man-made intelligence empowers customized growth opportunities by fitting instructive substance and exercises to individual understudy needs. Versatile learning stages influence artificial intelligence calculations to investigate understudy execution, distinguish learning designs, and powerfully change the trouble and speed of examples. This customized approach takes care of the different learning styles and capacities of understudies, cultivating a seriously captivating and compelling learning climate.

Keen Mentoring Frameworks:

Keen Mentoring Frameworks (ITS) influence man-made intelligence to offer individualized help to understudies. These frameworks can offer constant input, recognize areas of trouble, and adjust informative procedures to address explicit learning holes. By reproducing one-on-one mentoring encounters, ITS add to understudy dominance of subjects and the advancement of decisive reasoning abilities.

Information Driven Navigation:

Simulated intelligence examination and information driven experiences enable instructors and executives to pursue informed choices.

Dissecting information on understudy execution, participation, and commitment can assist with distinguishing regions for development, survey the viability of showing methodologies, and illuminate designated mediations. This information driven approach improves the general effectiveness of instructive establishments.

Computerized Authoritative Undertakings:

Man-made intelligence smoothes out authoritative undertakings, permitting instructors to zero in more on educating and less on administrative work. Robotized reviewing, planning, and routine regulatory cycles add to time reserve funds and functional productivity. This managerial help empowers teachers to devote additional opportunity to understudy cooperation, educational program improvement, and expert turn of events.

Virtual Study halls and Remote Learning:

Computer based intelligence assumes a critical part in the help of virtual homerooms and remote opportunities for growth. Man-made intelligence driven apparatuses, for example, video conferencing stages and cooperation programming, upgrade the openness of training, empowering understudies and teachers to interface flawlessly across geological limits. This has become especially critical with regards to worldwide occasions, for example, the Coronavirus pandemic, which sped up the reception of remote learning.

2. **Challenges in Schooling and simulated intelligence:**

While the mix of simulated intelligence in schooling offers groundbreaking open doors, it likewise presents difficulties that require cautious thought and moderation.

Moral Worries:

The utilization of simulated intelligence in training raises moral contemplations connected with information security, algorithmic predisposition, and the capable utilization of innovation. Gathering and investigating immense measures of understudy information require vigorous security shields to safeguard delicate data. Also, algorithmic predisposition in man-made intelligence frameworks might sustain existing disparities on the off chance that not tended to through cautious plan and checking.

Value and Access:

The computerized partition presents difficulties connected with value and access with regards to man-made intelligence driven instruction. Not all understudies have equivalent admittance to innovation, fast web, or gadgets important for successful support in computerized learning conditions. Overcoming this issue is fundamental to guarantee that the advantages of artificial intelligence upgraded training are open to all understudies, no matter what their financial foundation.

Overreliance on Innovation:

The incorporation of artificial intelligence ought to supplement, not supplant, successful instructing rehearses. Overreliance on innovation might obstruct the advancement of fundamental human abilities, like decisive reasoning, inventiveness, and relational correspondence. Finding some kind of harmony between utilizing artificial intelligence for effectiveness and safeguarding the humanistic parts of training is essential.

Instructor Readiness:

Viable coordination of computer based intelligence in training expects teachers to be knowledgeable in simulated intelligence ideas and applications. Numerous teachers might miss the mark on essential preparation and assets to successfully use simulated intelligence devices in their educating rehearses. Educator readiness and progressing proficient improvement are basic to amplifying the advantages of computer based intelligence in the homeroom.

Algorithmic Straightforwardness:

The absence of straightforwardness in computer based intelligence calculations presents difficulties in understanding how choices are made. Teachers, understudies, and guardians might be wary or worried about simulated intelligence driven dynamic cycles in training. Guaranteeing algorithmic straightforwardness is fundamental for building trust and addressing concerns connected with decency and responsibility.

3. **The Basic of simulated intelligence Proficiency in Training:**
   As simulated intelligence turns out to be progressively incorporated into instructive settings, the improvement of man-made intelligence proficiency becomes basic for understudies, instructors, and executives. Artificial intelligence education goes past specialized capability; it includes a comprehension of how man-made intelligence functions, its applications, and the moral contemplations related with its utilization.

Understudy computer based intelligence Education:

Understudies need to foster computer based intelligence education to actually explore the advanced scene. This incorporates grasping essential artificial intelligence ideas, perceiving the moral ramifications of artificial intelligence advances, and being basic shoppers of man-made intelligence driven content. Simulated intelligence proficiency enables understudies to draw in with innovation capably, cultivating an age of computerized residents who can contribute decidedly to society.

Instructor computer based intelligence Proficiency:

Teachers assume a focal part in forming understudies' computer based intelligence proficiency. Proficient improvement projects ought to zero in on furnishing instructors with the information and abilities expected to coordinate simulated intelligence advancements into their educating rehearses.

This includes understanding how to utilize computer based intelligence apparatuses, integrating them into the educational program, and encouraging decisive reasoning abilities connected with man-made intelligence.

Director simulated intelligence Proficiency:

Directors and policymakers in the schooling area likewise benefit from computer based intelligence education. This remembers understanding the likely effect of simulated intelligence for authoritative cycles, direction, and asset portion. Man-made intelligence proficient overseers can settle on informed decisions about the reception and execution of computer based intelligence innovations inside instructive establishments.

Moral Contemplations:

Man-made intelligence proficiency ought to accentuate the moral contemplations related with man-made intelligence advances. Understudies, instructors, and overseers should know about issues like security, predisposition, and the dependable utilization of information. Moral artificial intelligence proficiency advances a culture of dependable innovation use, guaranteeing that artificial intelligence is sent in manners that line up with cultural qualities and standards.

Decisive Reasoning Abilities:

Man-made intelligence education is firmly connected to the advancement of decisive reasoning abilities. Understudies ought to be urged to address and dissect the results of computer based intelligence calculations, figure out the impediments of man-made intelligence frameworks, and assess data produced by man-made intelligence. Sustaining a basic outlook empowers people to explore the intricacies of man-made intelligence driven data really.

4. **Systems for Encouraging artificial intelligence Proficiency in Schooling:**

Tending to the basic of man-made intelligence proficiency in training requires key drives that envelop educational plan advancement, proficient turn of events, and cooperative endeavors between instructive establishments, industry, and policymakers.

Integrating man-made intelligence into the Educational program:

Coordinate man-made intelligence ideas into the educational program across different subjects. This includes making modules that acquaint understudies with fundamental man-made intelligence standards, applications, and moral contemplations. Simulated intelligence ought to be treated as a cross-disciplinary subject that upgrades' comprehension understudies might interpret innovation's part in the public eye.

Proficient Improvement Projects:

Lay out proficient improvement programs for teachers that attention on computer based intelligence education.

These projects can give preparing on utilizing simulated intelligence apparatuses in the homeroom, coordinating simulated intelligence ideas into example plans, and cultivating conversations about moral contemplations. Joint efforts with industry specialists and man-made intelligence professionals can upgrade the adequacy of these projects.

Cooperation with Industry:

Cultivate cooperation between instructive foundations and industry accomplices to uncover understudies and teachers to genuine utilizations of simulated intelligence. Industry organizations can give admittance to artificial intelligence specialists, assets, and commonsense bits of knowledge that improve the instructive experience. Temporary position projects and visitor addresses from artificial intelligence experts add to a more thorough comprehension of man-made intelligence practically speaking.

Involved artificial intelligence Activities:

Draw in understudies in active artificial intelligence projects that empower trial and error and imagination. Building simulated intelligence models, creating straightforward calculations, or partaking in artificial intelligence related rivalries can demystify the innovation and impart trust in understudies. Commonsense encounters add to a more profound comprehension of computer based intelligence ideas.

Morals and Social Ramifications Conversations:

Consolidate conversations about the moral and social ramifications of artificial intelligence into the educational plan. Urge understudies to fundamentally break down contextual analyses, banter moral predicaments, and think about the cultural effect of simulated intelligence advances. These conversations encourage a feeling of obligation and mindfulness with respect to the more extensive ramifications of simulated intelligence.

Local area Commitment:

Stretch out computer based intelligence education drives to the more extensive local area. Studios, workshops, and effort projects can teach guardians, parental figures, and local area individuals about simulated intelligence proficiency. Building a local area that comprehends the job of simulated intelligence in training establishes a steady climate for understudies and teachers.

Deep rooted Learning Drives:

Perceive the unique idea of man-made intelligence and advance deep rooted learning drives for teachers and heads. Consistent learning open doors guarantee that instructive experts stay refreshed on the most recent advancements in man-made intelligence and can adjust their practices likewise.

5.3 Access to AI Technologies

The boundless accessibility and impartial admittance to Man-made brainpower (computer based intelligence) advancements have become basic contemplations in the developing scene of development, schooling, and cultural turn of events. As artificial intelligence keeps on penetrating different areas, including medical services, training, money, and industry, guaranteeing wide access becomes basic for forestalling innovation driven inconsistencies. This investigation digs into the multilayered parts of admittance to computer based intelligence innovations, analyzing difficulties, open doors, and the significance of cultivating comprehensive systems.

1. **Moves in Admittance to simulated intelligence Advancements:**

   Computerized Gap:

   The computerized partition, described by variations in admittance to innovation, stays a huge test in the fair dissemination of computer based intelligence innovations. Financial elements, geological area, and foundation limits add to differences in admittance to fast web, gadgets, and other mechanical assets. Spanning the computerized partition is fundamental to guarantee that people and networks have equivalent chances to outfit the advantages of simulated intelligence.

Cost and Reasonableness:

The expense related with man-made intelligence innovations, including equipment, programming, and talented work force, represents an obstruction to get to. Executing and keeping up with man-made intelligence frameworks can be monetarily difficult for people, independent companies, and associations with restricted assets. The moderateness of artificial intelligence advances should be addressed to forestall prohibition in view of monetary imperatives.

Ability Holes and Preparing:

The fruitful reception of simulated intelligence innovations requires a labor force with the important abilities to create, carry out, and deal with these frameworks. Be that as it may, there is a worldwide lack of talented experts in the field of computer based intelligence. Admittance to quality schooling and preparing programs is vital to connect the expertise holes and enable people to take part in the simulated intelligence driven economy.

Information Protection and Security Concerns:

Worries about information protection and security can go about as an obstacle to the far reaching reception of man-made intelligence innovations. People and associations might be hesitant to draw in with simulated intelligence frameworks on the off chance that there are worries about the treatment of delicate data.

Tending to these worries through hearty information insurance measures is fundamental for building trust and guaranteeing access for assorted client gatherings.

Administrative Boundaries:

Perplexing and prohibitive guidelines can obstruct the arrangement of computer based intelligence advancements, especially in areas with tough consistence necessities. Exploring administrative scenes can be trying for more modest organizations and new businesses, restricting their admittance to artificial intelligence driven arrangements. Smoothing out administrative systems and cultivating joint effort between administrative bodies and industry partners is urgent for guaranteeing dependable artificial intelligence reception.

2. **Valuable open doors for Admittance to computer based intelligence Advancements:**

Open Source and Cooperative Turn of events:

The open-source development and cooperative improvement drives play had a urgent impact in democratizing admittance to artificial intelligence advances. Open-source artificial intelligence structures, libraries, and apparatuses permit designers overall to get to and add to the advancement of state of the art computer based intelligence arrangements. This approach cultivates inclusivity by lessening obstructions to passage and empowering a worldwide local area of givers.

Distributed computing Administrations:

Distributed computing administrations have arisen as empowering agents of admittance to computer based intelligence advances, especially for associations with restricted framework abilities. Cloud-based artificial intelligence stages give adaptable and financially savvy arrangements, permitting organizations to use computer based intelligence abilities without huge forthright ventures. This model advances availability and adaptability in sending artificial intelligence applications.

Simulated intelligence Instruction and Preparing Projects:

Drives zeroed in on man-made intelligence schooling and preparing add to building a talented labor force and lessening the current expertise holes. Instructive projects, online courses, and certificates in artificial intelligence related fields enable people to get the information and aptitude expected to draw in with computer based intelligence advances. These projects assume a pivotal part in encouraging inclusivity by giving learning open doors to different socioeconomics.

Public-Private Associations:

Cooperative endeavors between people in general and confidential areas can upgrade admittance to artificial intelligence advancements.

Public-private organizations can prompt drives that address framework challenges, advance innovative work, and backing the arrangement of artificial intelligence arrangements in regions like medical care, training, and public administrations. These organizations influence the qualities of the two areas to make comprehensive and effective arrangements.

Comprehensive Development Centers:

Laying out development center points and hatcheries with an emphasis on inclusivity can encourage the turn of events and reception of computer based intelligence innovations. These center points give assets, mentorship, and backing to people and new businesses from different foundations, guaranteeing that an expansive range of trend-setters can add to the computer based intelligence biological system.

3. **Significance of man-made intelligence Proficiency:**
Enabling Clients:

Man-made intelligence proficiency, which incorporates understanding how simulated intelligence functions, its applications, and its effect on society, is significant for engaging clients. People with man-made intelligence education can pursue informed choices, basically survey computer based intelligence driven data, and effectively take part in the plan and sending of computer based intelligence advancements. Enabling clients through man-made intelligence education is a vital stage toward guaranteeing comprehensive access.

Lessening Dread and Doubt:

An absence of understanding about simulated intelligence innovations can add to dread and doubt. Man-made intelligence proficiency drives assist with demystifying man-made intelligence, explain its abilities and limits, and address misguided judgments. By lessening dread and encouraging a more educated viewpoint, simulated intelligence proficiency adds to more prominent acknowledgment and commitment with simulated intelligence innovations.

Working with Moral Use:

Man-made intelligence education remembers a comprehension of moral contemplations for man-made intelligence advancement and use. Teaching clients about the moral ramifications of computer based intelligence, including issues like inclination, security, and responsibility, advances mindful and moral utilization of simulated intelligence innovations. This information is fundamental for guaranteeing that computer based intelligence is conveyed in manners that line up with cultural qualities.

Advancing Comprehensive Turn of events:

Computer based intelligence education can add to advancing comprehensive improvement by empowering assorted support in artificial intelligence related fields.

At the point when people from various foundations, including underrepresented gatherings, have the information and abilities to draw in with man-made intelligence advances, it enhances the viewpoints and approaches in simulated intelligence improvement. Comprehensive improvement prompts arrangements that better location the requirements of different networks.

Progressing Deep rooted Learning:

The powerful idea of man-made intelligence requires a promise to long lasting learning. Artificial intelligence education drives support ceaseless learning and variation to mechanical headways.

By cultivating a culture of deep rooted learning, people can remain refreshed on the most recent improvements in computer based intelligence, guaranteeing that they stay dynamic members in the developing advanced scene.

4. **Methodologies for Encouraging Comprehensive Access:**

1. **Framework Improvement:**

Put resources into framework improvement to address the computerized partition. This incorporates extending fast web access, guaranteeing reasonable network, and giving admittance to gadgets in underserved regions. Government drives and confidential area joint efforts can assume an essential part in building the vital framework for far and wide access.

2. **Instruction and Preparing Drives:**

Carry out thorough schooling and preparing drives that attention on computer based intelligence proficiency. These drives ought to be intended to arrive at assorted socioeconomics, including understudies, experts, and people in non-specialized fields. Team up with instructive foundations, industry accomplices, and local area associations to convey available and significant computer based intelligence schooling.

3. **Comprehensive Innovative work:**

Energize and uphold innovative work endeavors that focus on inclusivity. This includes advancing variety in simulated intelligence research groups, tending to predisposition in man-made intelligence calculations, and guaranteeing that computer based intelligence advancements are intended to serve assorted client gatherings. Comprehensive Research and development rehearses add to the formation of computer based intelligence arrangements that are more agent and fair.

4. **Public Mindfulness Missions:**

Send off open mindfulness missions to demystify computer based intelligence and convey its advantages. These missions ought to feature certifiable uses of man-made intelligence, dissipate fantasies, and accentuate the positive effect of artificial intelligence on different areas. Public mindfulness adds to a more educated and responsive crowd, encouraging an uplifting outlook toward simulated intelligence innovations.

5. **Joint effort between Areas:**

Encourage joint effort between government, industry, the scholarly community, and non-benefit associations to make all encompassing answers for comprehensive access. Multi-sectoral joint efforts can address difficulties exhaustively, utilizing the qualities and assets of every area. Drives, for example, joint examination projects, information sharing stages, and limit building projects can result from compelling coordinated effort.

6

Chapter 6

Government Regulations and Policies

Unofficial laws and strategies assume an essential part in molding the scene of Computerized reasoning (man-made intelligence) improvement, sending, and use. As computer based intelligence advances keep on propelling, legislatures all over the planet are confronted with the test of laying out systems that offset development with moral contemplations, protection concerns, and cultural effect. This investigation digs into the complex parts of unofficial laws and strategies in the domain of man-made intelligence, looking at the key contemplations, developing patterns, and the basic of establishing a favorable administrative climate.

1. **Key Contemplations in artificial intelligence Guidelines:**
   Moral Rules:
   Moral contemplations are foremost in the turn of events and organization of simulated intelligence advancements. State run administrations are progressively perceiving the need to lay out moral rules that oversee simulated intelligence frameworks.
   These rules address issues like reasonableness, straightforwardness, responsibility, and the evasion of predisposition in artificial

intelligence calculations. Moral systems plan to guarantee that simulated intelligence advances line up with cultural qualities and don't coincidentally propagate separation or damage.

Security Assurance:

Man-made intelligence frequently includes the handling and investigation of tremendous measures of information, raising worries about protection. Legislatures are establishing guidelines to defend people's protection privileges with regards to simulated intelligence applications. This incorporates guidelines indicating how individual information can be gathered, put away, and utilized, as well as systems for acquiring assent from people. Security assurance measures are significant to fabricate trust in computer based intelligence frameworks and moderate the gamble of unapproved information use.

Straightforwardness and Logic:

The absence of straightforwardness in man-made intelligence calculations has been a subject of concern. Legislatures are underscoring the significance of straightforwardness and logic in artificial intelligence frameworks, especially in applications that influence people's lives. Guidelines might expect associations to unveil how computer based intelligence choices are made, empowering clients to figure out the reasoning behind algorithmic results. This straightforwardness cultivates responsibility and helps address concerns connected with algorithmic inclination.

Security and Responsibility:

Security contemplations are fundamental to artificial intelligence guidelines, particularly in basic spaces like medical care, finance, and independent frameworks. State run administrations are creating approaches that order powerful network safety measures to shield man-made intelligence frameworks from malignant assaults and unapproved access. Moreover, responsibility measures guarantee that associations sending computer based intelligence advancements are considered liable for the results of their frameworks, especially in examples where mischief might happen.

Fair Contest and Market Elements:

Guidelines in the man-made intelligence space additionally expect to cultivate fair rivalry and forestall hostile to cutthroat practices. State run administrations might set rules to guarantee that artificial intelligence markets are open, serious, and helpful for development. This includes resolving issues like monopolistic way of behaving, information syndications, and guaranteeing that more modest endeavors have a level battleground in the artificial intelligence biological system.

Global Cooperation:

Given the worldwide idea of simulated intelligence advancement and arrangement, legislatures are progressively perceiving the significance of global coordinated effort in forming administrative systems. Cooperative endeavors include sharing prescribed procedures, laying out normal principles, and tending to difficulties that rise above public lines. Worldwide cooperation is significant to making a fit methodology that works with moral computer based intelligence improvement on a worldwide scale.

2. **Developing Patterns in simulated intelligence Guidelines:**

Area Explicit Guidelines:

As simulated intelligence applications become more particular and different, there is a pattern towards area explicit guidelines. Various ventures, like medical services, finance, and independent vehicles, present interesting difficulties and require customized administrative methodologies. Area explicit guidelines empower specialists to address the subtleties and explicit dangers related with computer based intelligence arrangement in different spaces.

Dynamic and Versatile Guidelines:

The quick speed of artificial intelligence progressions requires administrative systems that are dynamic and versatile. Legislatures are creating some distance from static guidelines to embrace more spry methodologies that can stay up with mechanical turns of events. This includes the fuse of components that take into account nonstop checking, updates, and acclimations to guidelines in light of the developing scene of simulated intelligence.

Administrative Sandboxes:

Administrative sandboxes are arising as a clever way to deal with encourage development in simulated intelligence while keeping up with administrative oversight. These sandboxes give controlled conditions where organizations can test man-made intelligence applications under the oversight of administrative specialists. This empowers controllers to grasp the viable ramifications of computer based intelligence advancements, recognize expected chances, and cooperatively foster successful administrative measures.

Algorithmic Effect Appraisals:

Legislatures are investigating the execution of algorithmic effect evaluations as a feature of administrative cycles. These appraisals include assessing the possible effect of artificial intelligence calculations on different elements, including protection, reasonableness, and cultural prosperity. Integrating algorithmic effect evaluations distinguishes and address expected takes a chance before computer based intelligence frameworks are sent at scale.

Public Conference and Support:

Perceiving the cultural ramifications of man-made intelligence, states are progressively including general society in the administrative cycle. Public conference systems, like open hearings and criticism meetings, permit residents to communicate their perspectives on artificial intelligence guidelines. This participatory methodology guarantees that different points of view are thought of, adding to additional comprehensive and compelling administrative systems.

Worldwide Principles and Interoperability:

Endeavors to lay out worldwide principles for computer based intelligence are picking up speed. States are participating in global discussions to foster normal principles that advance interoperability and similarity among computer based intelligence frameworks. Worldwide principles add to consistency in administrative methodologies, work with cross-line coordinated efforts, and lessen obstructions to the global sending of artificial intelligence advancements.

3. **Basic of Establishing a Favorable Administrative Climate: Adjusting Development and Chance Relief:**
The basic of establishing a helpful administrative climate lies in finding some kind of harmony between encouraging development and relieving gambles. Legislatures intend to make systems that support the turn of events and reception of computer based intelligence advances while shielding against expected hurts. Adjusting these needs requires a nuanced comprehension of the developing mechanical scene and proactive administrative measures.

Building Trust and Responsibility:
A favorable administrative climate is fundamental for building trust in artificial intelligence innovations. Clear guidelines, moral rules, and responsibility systems add to a straightforward and dependable simulated intelligence environment. Trust is a fundamental component that supports clients, organizations, and policymakers to embrace artificial intelligence advancements with trust in their capable turn of events and use.

Guaranteeing Inclusivity and Openness:
Guidelines ought to be intended to guarantee inclusivity and openness in the sending of computer based intelligence advancements. This includes resolving issues connected with the advanced separation, guaranteeing that simulated intelligence benefits are available to assorted populaces, and staying away from the formation of innovation driven inconsistencies. Comprehensive guidelines add to evenhanded admittance to the potential open doors

introduced by man-made intelligence.

Adjusting to Mechanical Progressions:

A favorable administrative climate is one that can adjust to the quick speed of innovative progressions. Guidelines should be adequately adaptable to oblige new turns of events, arising use cases, and unexpected difficulties. This flexibility requires progressing joint effort between administrative bodies, industry partners, and the examination local area.

Empowering Mindful artificial intelligence Advancement:

The administrative climate ought to empower dependable artificial intelligence advancement rehearses. This incorporates advancing straightforwardness, logic, reasonableness, and responsibility in computer based intelligence frameworks. Administrative systems ought to boost associations to focus on moral contemplations and mindful artificial intelligence rehearses all through the advancement lifecycle.

Working with Cross-Area Cooperation:

Coordinated effort between various areas, including government, industry, the scholarly world, and common society, is urgent for the outcome of simulated intelligence guidelines. Cross-area joint effort guarantees that guidelines are educated by assorted points of view, benefit from aggregate aptitude, and are lined up with more extensive cultural objectives. Open discourse and joint effort add to the improvement of comprehensive and viable administrative structures.

4. **Worldwide Points of view on artificial intelligence Guidelines:**
European Association (EU):

The EU has been at the very front of artificial intelligence guideline, with the presentation of the Man-made reasoning Demonstration. The Demonstration frames a gamble based approach, ordering simulated intelligence frameworks into various gamble levels and forcing explicit necessities in light of the gamble they present. It resolves issues like straightforwardness, responsibility, and information utilization, underscoring the assurance of major freedoms.

US:

In the US, there is a developing acknowledgment of the requirement for government artificial intelligence guidelines. While the methodology has been more area explicit, there is expanding energy for extensive regulation. Different states have previously instituted or proposed man-made intelligence related regulations, and conversations at the government level plan to make a strong administrative system.

China:

China has focused on simulated intelligence improvement as a public procedure and has given rules and strategies to manage its utilization. The accentuation is on cultivating development and seriousness in man-made intelligence, however there are additionally endeavors to lay out moral rules and information assurance guidelines. China's administrative methodology mirrors its obligation to turning into a worldwide simulated intelligence pioneer.

Canada:

Canada has adopted a cooperative strategy to computer based intelligence guideline, including partners from industry, the scholarly community, and common society. The Canadian government has stressed the significance of mindful computer based intelligence advancement and moral contemplations. Drives center around advancing straightforwardness, reasonableness, and inclusivity in artificial intelligence frameworks.

Worldwide Joint effort:

Universally, there are endeavors to cultivate cooperation and lay out normal standards for computer based intelligence guideline. Associations like the OECD (Association for Financial Co-activity and Advancement) and the G20 have been making progress toward worldwide agreement on artificial intelligence administration. Cooperative drives mean to make a mutual perspective of moral simulated intelligence improvement and sending.

5. Future Bearings and Difficulties:

Tending to Inclination and Decency:

A basic test in simulated intelligence guidelines is tending to predisposition and guaranteeing decency in simulated intelligence frameworks. As simulated intelligence calculations gain from verifiable information, there is a gamble of propagating existing inclinations. Future guidelines should zero in on alleviating predisposition, advancing reasonableness, and carrying out measures to correct differences in simulated intelligence results.

Controlling computer based intelligence in Independent Frameworks:

The ascent of independent frameworks, including self-driving vehicles and robots, presents interesting administrative difficulties. Future guidelines should address wellbeing, responsibility, and moral contemplations in the organization of simulated intelligence in independent frameworks. Finding some kind of harmony among development and guaranteeing public wellbeing will be a key concentration.

Global Harmonization:

Accomplishing global harmonization in man-made intelligence guidelines stays a perplexing undertaking. While there are endeavors towards normal standards, administrative uniqueness among nations endures. The test lies in accommodating different lawful customs, social viewpoints, and ways to deal with administration. Future headings might include expanded coordinated effort and the improvement of components for blending worldwide computer based intelligence guidelines.

Expecting to arise Innovations:

The administrative scene should be ready to expect and address arising innovations inside the artificial intelligence area.

As man-made intelligence keeps on advancing, new applications and standards, like quantum computer based intelligence and neurotechnology, will introduce novel difficulties. Guidelines should be forward-looking and versatile to the advancing mechanical scene.

Guaranteeing Public Getting it:

Future bearings in computer based intelligence guidelines ought to incorporate drives to upgrade public comprehension of simulated intelligence. As artificial intelligence frameworks become more predominant in day to day existence, it is vital for people to have an essential comprehension of how computer based intelligence functions, its applications, and possible ramifications. Instructive missions and mindfulness projects can add to informed public talk on simulated intelligence guidelines.

6.1 Current Regulatory Landscape

The ongoing administrative scene encompassing Computerized reasoning (simulated intelligence) is set apart by a complicated interchange of endeavors to saddle the expected advantages of man-made intelligence while tending to its moral, legitimate, and cultural ramifications. States and administrative bodies overall are wrestling with the unique idea of simulated intelligence advancements, attempting to work out some kind of harmony between advancing development and protecting against likely dangers. This investigation dives into the multi-layered parts of the ongoing administrative scene, enveloping provincial methodologies, key administrative systems, and the difficulties looked in administering computer based intelligence.

1. **Provincial Ways to deal with man-made intelligence Guideline:**

   European Association (EU):

   The European Association has arisen as a pioneer in laying out complete guidelines to oversee computer based intelligence. The proposed Man-made reasoning Demonstration, divulged by the European Commission in April 2021, means to make an orchestrated administrative system for computer based intelligence sending across EU part states. The Demonstration arranges man-made intelligence frameworks into various gamble classifications, going from inadmissible gamble to insignificant gamble, and presents relating commitments for designers and clients. Prominent arrangements incorporate prerequisites for straightforwardness, human oversight, and severe disallowances on specific high-risk simulated intelligence applications. The proposed guidelines mirror the EU's obligation to encouraging moral simulated intelligence advancement and guaranteeing the assurance of essential privileges.

US:

The administrative scene for simulated intelligence in the US is described by a more decentralized approach, with different government organizations investigating area explicit guidelines. The Public Foundation of Guidelines and Innovation (NIST) has been effectively engaged with creating simulated intelligence norms, while organizations, for example, the Government Exchange Commission (FTC) center around customer security and protection concerns. Also, individual states, including California, have sanctioned or proposed regulation tending to explicit parts of computer based intelligence, like inclination relief and algorithmic straightforwardness. The shortfall of an exhaustive government system has prompted an interwoven of guidelines, inciting progressing conversations about the requirement for general regulation to address the more extensive range of computer based intelligence applications.

China:

China has focused on simulated intelligence improvement as an essential public goal, planning to turn into a worldwide forerunner in the field. While administrative endeavors in China principally center around encouraging development and seriousness, there are likewise drives to lay out moral rules and information security guidelines. The Chinese government has delivered rules for the turn of events and arrangement of simulated intelligence innovations, underscoring dependable computer based intelligence rehearses. The methodology mirrors China's obligation to adjusting the advancement of mechanical progressions with moral contemplations and lining up with worldwide norms.

Canada:

Canada has taken on a cooperative way to deal with man-made intelligence administration, including partners from government, industry, the scholarly community, and common society. The Canadian government has given a bunch of moral rules for man-made intelligence improvement, stressing straightforwardness, decency, responsibility, and inclusivity. Drives, for example, the Skillet Canadian Computerized reasoning Methodology and the Canadian simulated intelligence Morals Working Gathering exhibit a promise to dependable artificial intelligence improvement. While Canada's administrative methodology is portrayed by standards and joint effort, conversations around formal regulation are continuous.

2. **Key Administrative Structures:**

EU's Man-made consciousness Act:

The EU's proposed Man-made consciousness Act is a milestone administrative structure that intends to lay out a brought together way to deal with computer based intelligence administration across the part states. The Demonstration arranges artificial intelligence frameworks into three gamble levels: inadmissible gamble, high gamble, and negligible gamble.

High-risk applications, like basic framework, biometric recognizable proof, and instructive man-made intelligence frameworks, face severe prerequisites, including congruity evaluations, human oversight, and straightforwardness commitments. The Demonstration additionally denies specific purposes of computer based intelligence that present critical dangers, for example, social scoring and ongoing remote biometric recognizable proof for policing.

NIST's simulated intelligence Norms:

The Public Establishment of Norms and Innovation (NIST) in the US has been effectively engaged with creating principles and rules for artificial intelligence. NIST's methodology centers around tending to the specialized difficulties related with simulated intelligence, including logic, dependability, and strength. The NIST simulated intelligence norms expect to give an establishment to interoperability, unwavering quality, and the capable utilization of artificial intelligence innovations. While these guidelines are not legitimately restricting, they act as a source of perspective for industry experts, policymakers, and specialists.

OECD's man-made intelligence Standards:

The Association for Monetary Co-activity and Improvement (OECD) has laid out a bunch of simulated intelligence rules that guide part nations in creating artificial intelligence strategies. The OECD simulated intelligence standards incorporate regions like straightforwardness, responsibility, and inclusivity. The standards underscore the requirement for human-driven artificial intelligence frameworks and stress the significance of encouraging worldwide joint effort to address worldwide difficulties related with man-made intelligence. While not lawfully restricting, the OECD standards act as a structure for nations to adjust their public man-made intelligence systems to shared values.

China's artificial intelligence Rules:

China has given rules for the turn of events and organization of simulated intelligence advancements, framing standards for capable artificial intelligence rehearses. The rules underline the significance of reasonableness, straightforwardness, and responsibility in artificial intelligence frameworks. While China's way to deal with computer based intelligence guideline is portrayed by an emphasis on development and seriousness, these rules signal a promise to moral contemplations in simulated intelligence improvement. The rules additionally address issues connected with information security, client protection, and the capable utilization of man-made intelligence in different areas.

3. **Challenges in Administering artificial intelligence:**
Speed of Mechanical Progressions:
One of the first difficulties in administering artificial intelligence lies in the quick speed of mechanical progressions. Conventional administrative structures battle to stay aware of the powerful idea of artificial intelligence developments.

As man-made intelligence advances develop, controllers face the test of adjusting and refreshing guidelines to address arising use cases, applications, and likely dangers.

Absence of Worldwide Agreement:
The absence of a worldwide agreement on man-made intelligence guidelines represents a critical test. Shifting administrative methodologies across locales and nations can prompt administrative fracture, blocking global joint effort and the improvement of normal guidelines. Accomplishing worldwide arrangement on major standards and principles stays a complicated undertaking, requiring facilitated endeavors from the global local area.

Inclination and Reasonableness Concerns:
Tending to predisposition and reasonableness worries in artificial intelligence calculations is a persevering test. As computer based intelligence frameworks gain from authentic information, they might sustain existing predispositions and add to unreasonable results. Controllers face the test of laying out structures that advance reasonableness, straightforwardness, and responsibility in computer based intelligence frameworks, with an emphasis on relieving predisposition and guaranteeing evenhanded artificial intelligence applications.

Interdisciplinary Nature of computer based intelligence:
The interdisciplinary idea of artificial intelligence, spreading

over software engineering, morals, regulation, and sociologies, presents administrative difficulties. Successful man-made intelligence administration requires cooperation between specialists from different fields to foster comprehensive systems that address specialized, moral, and cultural aspects. Controllers should explore the intricacy of interdisciplinary contemplations to make complete and nuanced guidelines.

Adjusting Advancement and Guideline:

Finding some kind of harmony between cultivating development and carrying out compelling guidelines is a sensitive test. Overregulation can smother innovative progressions and prevent the advancement of man-made intelligence applications with groundbreaking potential. Then again, lacking guideline might prompt moral slips, protection breaks, and different dangers related with uncontrolled artificial intelligence organization. Controllers should cautiously explore this equilibrium to establish a climate that supports dependable development.

Moral and Cultural Ramifications:

The moral and cultural ramifications of computer based intelligence add intricacy to administrative contemplations. Controllers should wrestle with questions connected with the effect of computer based intelligence on business, protection, and individual privileges. Moral structures, for example, those tending to the utilization of man-made intelligence in delicate applications like law enforcement, medical services, and schooling, require cautious thought to guarantee that guidelines line up with cultural qualities and assumptions.

4. **Future Headings in simulated intelligence Guideline:**

Harmonization Endeavors:

Future headings in artificial intelligence guideline are probably going to include expanded endeavors towards harmonization. Cooperative drives pointed toward making normal guidelines and standards for man-made intelligence administration will be pivotal. Worldwide associations, states, and industry partners might pursue adjusting administrative ways to deal with cultivate consistency and work with the dependable turn of events and sending of simulated intelligence on a worldwide scale.

Dynamic and Versatile Guidelines:

Perceiving the powerful idea of man-made intelligence innovations, future guidelines are supposed to embrace a more unique and versatile methodology. Adaptable structures that can develop in light of mechanical progressions, arising gambles, and cultural changes will be fundamental. Administrative bodies might integrate systems for persistent observing, updates, and acclimations to stay up with the developing scene of computer based intelligence.

Morals Driven Guidelines:

There is a developing accentuation on morals driven guidelines that focus on mindful computer based intelligence improvement. Future guidelines might put more prominent significance on straightforwardness, reasonableness, and decency in artificial intelligence frameworks. Moral contemplations, including the anticipation of predisposition and segregation, are probably going to be installed into administrative structures to guarantee that simulated intelligence lines up with cultural qualities and standards.

Public Cooperation and Mindfulness:

Future bearings in artificial intelligence guideline might include expanded public cooperation and mindfulness. Consideration of public points of view in the administrative cycle, through components like public counsels and partner commitment, can add to additional agent and responsible guidelines. Bringing issues to light about artificial intelligence and its suggestions will enable people to take part in informed conversations on administrative issues.

Cross-Area Cooperation:

Cooperation between areas, including government, industry, the scholarly community, and common society, will be fundamental for viable computer based intelligence guideline. Cross-area cooperation can use different ability to foster exhaustive administrative systems that address the interdisciplinary idea of artificial intelligence. Open exchange and shared assets will add to more strong and comprehensive administration of computer based intelligence advancements.

6.2 International Collaboration and Standards

Worldwide cooperation and the foundation of principles are critical components in molding the capable turn of events, sending, and administration of Man-made consciousness (man-made intelligence) on a worldwide scale. As man-made intelligence advances rise above public boundaries, the requirement for cooperative endeavors and shared guidelines becomes basic. This investigation digs into the diverse scene of global coordinated effort in computer based intelligence, featuring the job of associations, drives, and the difficulties in laying out normal principles that encourage development while tending to moral, lawful, and cultural contemplations.

1. **Worldwide Associations and Drives:**
   Association for Financial Co-activity and Advancement (OECD):
   The OECD has been at the front of global endeavors to lay out normal standards for computer based intelligence administration. The OECD man-made intelligence Standards, took on in 2019, give an extensive structure that stresses values like straightforwardness, responsibility, and inclusivity. Part nations focus on sticking to these standards, which act as an establishment for molding public computer based intelligence strategies. The OECD additionally works with conversations on computer based intelligence related difficulties and best practices through drives like the OECD artificial intelligence Strategy Observatory.
   Worldwide Organization on Computerized reasoning (GPAI):
   Sent off in 2020, the GPAI is a global drive that expects to cultivate cooperation on simulated intelligence research, strategy

improvement, and execution. The GPAI comprises of establishing individuals from different locales, including Canada, France, Germany, India, Japan, the Unified Realm, and the US. The drive centers around addressing difficulties connected with dependable simulated intelligence advancement, including protection, security, and basic freedoms. By uniting states, industry, and the scholarly world, the GPAI tries to pool aptitude and assets to support the worldwide local area.

Joined Countries (UN):

The Unified Countries assumes a pivotal part in working with worldwide conversations on artificial intelligence administration. The UN's Middle for Man-made brainpower and Mechanical technology (UNICRI) attempts to advance the capable utilization of computer based intelligence innovations and address related chances. The UN's work incorporates investigating the moral ramifications of simulated intelligence in different areas, advancing common freedoms in computer based intelligence advancement, and encouraging worldwide collaboration. The UN fills in as a stage for part states to share points of view and team up on molding the moral and legitimate parts of artificial intelligence.

Worldwide Media transmission Association (ITU):

The ITU, a specific organization of the Unified Countries, effectively adds to worldwide endeavors on simulated intelligence normalization. The ITU's Emphasis Gathering on simulated intelligence for Wellbeing is an illustration of cooperative endeavors to normalize man-made intelligence applications in a particular space. By assembling specialists from around the world, the ITU plans to foster structures that advance interoperability, moral contemplations, and the mindful arrangement of simulated intelligence innovations.

2. **Normal Standards and Principles:**
   OECD man-made intelligence Standards:

The OECD man-made intelligence Standards act as a basic structure for capable simulated intelligence improvement and organization. The standards envelop values like reasonableness, straightforwardness, responsibility, and human-driven plan. Part nations focus on carrying out these standards in their public man-made intelligence strategies, adding to a mutual perspective of moral contemplations. The OECD standards give a shared view to nations to adjust their ways to deal with computer based intelligence administration and advance capable development.

ISO/IEC Guidelines:

The Worldwide Association for Normalization (ISO) and the Global Electrotechnical Commission (IEC) team up to foster global guidelines for man-made intelligence. The ISO/IEC JTC 1/SC 42 board of trustees centers around normalization in the field of man-made intelligence, covering viewpoints like wording, systems, and morals. Norms like ISO/IEC 23053 give rules to the administration of man-made intelligence, adding to an orchestrated way to deal with artificial intelligence improvement and organization across various businesses and areas.

IEEE Worldwide Drive on Morals of Independent and Savvy Frameworks:

The Foundation of Electrical and Gadgets Designers (IEEE) has laid out drives zeroed in on the moral contemplations of artificial intelligence. The IEEE Worldwide Drive on Morals of Independent and Smart Frameworks has fostered the Morally Adjusted Plan series, which gives a structure to the moral plan and sending of computer based intelligence innovations. By connecting with a worldwide local area of specialists, IEEE adds to the foundation of moral norms that rise above public limits.

GPAI's Functioning Gatherings:

The Worldwide Organization on Man-made consciousness has laid out working gatherings that attention on unambiguous subjects, including capable man-made intelligence, information

administration, and computer based intelligence in training.
These functioning gatherings unite specialists from various locales to team up on creating systems and rules. The results of the functioning gatherings add to the foundation of worldwide norms that address assorted parts of artificial intelligence administration.

3. **Challenges in Global Cooperation and Normalization:**
Disparate Public Strategies:

One of the huge difficulties in global joint effort is the presence of disparate public arrangements and administrative structures. Nations might move toward simulated intelligence administration in view of their remarkable social, lawful, and monetary contemplations. Spanning these divergences and cultivating a typical comprehension requires political endeavors and progressing exchange to settle on some mutual interest while regarding the power of individual countries.

Moral and Social Inconstancy:

Man-made intelligence principles should explore moral and social fluctuation across districts. What might be viewed as moral in one social setting would contrast in another. Tending to these varieties requires a nuanced approach that obliges different points of view on moral contemplations, protection standards, and cultural qualities. Accomplishing an equilibrium that regards social contrasts while maintaining basic standards represents a complicated test.

Innovation and Strategy Misalignment:

The quick speed of innovative headways frequently outperforms the advancement of relating approaches and norms. Thus, there can be a misalignment between the capacities of man-made intelligence advances and the administrative structures set up. Finding some kind of harmony that considers development while guaranteeing capable use requires nimbleness in arrangement making and worldwide joint effort to stay up with mechanical advancement.

Implementation and Consistence:

Laying out global principles is just essential for the test; guaranteeing requirement and consistence across different wards is similarly intricate. Nations might have shifting capacities with respect to implementation, and the absence of an incorporated overseeing body for worldwide simulated intelligence principles makes it trying to guarantee reliable consistence. Instruments for observing and implementing guidelines on a worldwide scale remain regions that request consideration.

Inclusivity and Portrayal:

Global coordinated effort requires inclusivity and portrayal from a different scope of nations and partners. Guaranteeing that the viewpoints, everything being equal, especially those from arising economies, are considered is indispensable for making norms that mirror a worldwide agreement. Challenges connected with asset abberations, language boundaries, and openness should be addressed to encourage genuinely comprehensive joint effort.

4. **Future Bearings in Worldwide Cooperation and Principles:**

Worldwide Administration Systems:

Future headings in worldwide coordinated effort might include investigating worldwide administration systems for man-made intelligence. Endeavors to lay out worldwide establishments or arrangements that supervise computer based intelligence norms and strategies on a worldwide scale could upgrade coordination and make a more firm way to deal with tending to moral, lawful, and cultural contemplations. Such instruments would should be intended to oblige different points of view and advance impartial portrayal.

Limit Building and Schooling:

Reinforcing limit building and instructive drives is pivotal for cultivating worldwide joint effort. Enabling nations, especially those with restricted assets, to effectively partake in conversations on man-made intelligence norms and administration requires interests in schooling, preparing, and the advancement of skill. Drives that span the information hole and assemble the capacities of assorted partners will add to additional educated and comprehensive joint efforts.

Public-Private Organizations:

Empowering public-private organizations can improve coordinated effort on artificial intelligence guidelines. Industry partners, state run administrations, and common society associations assume corresponding parts in forming the man-made intelligence scene. Cooperative drives that unite these different elements can prompt the improvement of guidelines that are in fact vigorous as well as intelligent of an expansive range of points of view and interests.

Multi-Partner Commitment:

Future bearings ought to include a proceeded with accentuation on multi-partner commitment. Comprehensive discourse that incorporates legislatures, industry, the scholarly community, common society, and global associations guarantees an all encompassing way to deal with man-made intelligence administration. Components like discussions, working gatherings, and cooperative activities that work with open correspondence and joint effort will be instrumental in molding worldwide guidelines.

Coordinated and Versatile Methodologies:

Perceiving the unique idea of man-made intelligence advancements, future worldwide coordinated efforts should take on spry and versatile methodologies. Guidelines and administration structures ought to be intended to develop with mechanical progressions, arising difficulties, and cultural changes. Laying out components for continuous surveys, updates, and changes will guarantee that global principles stay applicable and viable.

6.3 Future Policy Considerations

As the field of Man-made reasoning (simulated intelligence) keeps on developing at a fast speed, future strategy contemplations become progressively basic to guarantee the mindful turn of events, organization, and administration of simulated intelligence innovations. Policymakers face the test of finding some kind of harmony between encouraging development and tending to moral, lawful, and cultural ramifications. This investigation dives into key future strategy contemplations that ought to be at the front of conversations to direct the development of man-made intelligence in a way that benefits humankind while relieving expected gambles.

1. **Moral Rules and Human-Driven man-made intelligence:**
   Moral man-made intelligence Improvement:
   Future strategies should accentuate the significance of moral man-made intelligence improvement. Policymakers ought to team up with artificial intelligence scientists, industry partners, and ethicists to lay out clear moral rules that focus on straight-forwardness, decency, responsibility, and human-driven plan. Empowering mindful practices in artificial intelligence advancement will add to the making of frameworks that line up with cultural qualities and regard individual privileges.
   Human-Driven Plan:
   Approaches ought to advocate for human-driven simulated intelligence configuration, setting human prosperity, independence, and pride at the center of advancement. Consolidating client driven viewpoints and including different partners in the plan cycle will assist with making computer based intelligence frameworks that are natural, available, and circumspect of the requirements and inclinations of end-clients. Human-driven plan standards can relieve the possible adverse consequence of man-made intelligence on people and networks.

2. **Guideline and Administration:**
   Exhaustive Administrative Systems:
   Future arrangements ought to zero in on creating extensive administrative structures that address the developing scene of man-made intelligence. These structures ought to cover different areas,

including information security, algorithmic straightforwardness, and responsibility for man-made intelligence framework results. Finding some kind of harmony between empowering development and shielding against potential damages requires nuanced guidelines that are versatile to mechanical progressions.

Risk-Based Approaches:

Policymakers ought to consider taking on risk-based ways to deal with artificial intelligence guideline. Distinguishing and classifying artificial intelligence applications in light of the degree of chance they present considers custom-made administrative necessities. High-risk applications, like those in medical care or independent frameworks, may warrant more rigid guidelines, while okay applications can profit from a more adaptable administrative climate that cultivates development.

3. **Straightforwardness and Logic:**

Algorithmic Straightforwardness:

Strategies ought to accentuate the significance of algorithmic straightforwardness, particularly in applications that influence people's lives. Guaranteeing that computer based intelligence frameworks are straightforward permits clients to comprehend the dynamic cycles and considers designers responsible for likely inclinations or biased results. Straightforwardness additionally encourages trust between clients, engineers, and administrative bodies.

Logic in simulated intelligence Frameworks:

Future strategies ought to address the test of artificial intelligence framework reasonableness. Guaranteeing that simulated intelligence frameworks can give reasonable clarifications to their choices is essential, especially in areas like medical care, money, and law enforcement. Logic upgrades client trust as well as takes into account better examination of computer based intelligence applications, empowering the ID and rectification of possible predispositions or blunders.

4. **Information Administration and Security:**
Information Insurance Guidelines:

Policymakers ought to keep on fortifying information assurance guidelines to defend people's security in the time of artificial intelligence. Stricter principles with respect to the assortment, stockpiling, and utilization of individual information can relieve the gamble of protection breaks and unapproved access. Strategies ought to likewise address the difficulties presented by the rising volume of information created by man-made intelligence applications.

Client Assent and Control:

Future arrangements ought to underline the significance of client assent and command over private information. People ought to reserve the option to comprehend how their information is being utilized and the capacity to give or renounce assent for its utilization. Strategies that enable clients to control their information add to a more moral and protection regarding simulated intelligence environment.

5. **Worldwide Coordinated effort:**
Harmonization of Principles:

Policymakers ought to effectively participate in global joint effort to blend man-made intelligence guidelines. Cooperative endeavors with different countries, associations, and partners can prompt the improvement of worldwide norms that work with interoperability and reliable administration. Harmonization diminishes discontinuity and guarantees a more firm way to deal with simulated intelligence guideline on the world stage.

Worldwide Administration Systems:

Thought ought to be given to the foundation of worldwide administration instruments for man-made intelligence. While regarding the sway of individual countries, making worldwide foundations or arrangements that direct simulated intelligence norms and strategies on a worldwide scale can upgrade coordination, data sharing, and the improvement of generally acknowledged moral rules.

6. **Inclusivity and Variety:**

Comprehensive computer based intelligence Advancement:

Future arrangements ought to empower comprehensive simulated intelligence advancement that thinks about different viewpoints. Policymakers ought to advance drives that guarantee the consideration of underrepresented bunches in simulated intelligence innovative work. A different labor force adds to the production of computer based intelligence frameworks that are not so much one-sided but rather more intelligent of the more extensive populace.

Tending to Inclination and Reasonableness:

Strategies ought to expressly address the test of predisposition and decency in artificial intelligence frameworks. Guaranteeing that man-made intelligence applications don't propagate or intensify existing cultural inclinations requires proactive measures. Policymakers ought to advocate for the utilization of different and delegate datasets, algorithmic reviews, and progressing observing to distinguish and correct one-sided results.

7. **Instruction and Labor force Advancement:**

Artificial intelligence Education Projects:

Policymakers ought to put resources into computer based intelligence proficiency projects to improve public comprehension of computer based intelligence advances. Training drives that give people the information and abilities to explore the man-made intelligence scene add to informed direction, moral contemplations, and capable utilization of man-made intelligence in day to day existence.

Upskilling and Reskilling:

Future strategies ought to focus on upskilling and reskilling projects to set up the labor force for the changing requests of the man-made intelligence driven economy. As simulated intelligence advances reshape businesses and occupation jobs, putting resources into constant learning valuable open doors guarantees that people can adjust to new difficulties and partake in the advantages of artificial intelligence driven development.

8. **Responsibility and Obligation:**

Clear Responsibility Systems:

Policymakers ought to lay out clear responsibility instruments for man-made intelligence frameworks. Characterizing jobs and obligations, particularly on account of independent frameworks, guarantees that there is a structure for considering people and associations responsible for the activities and results of man-made intelligence innovations.

Risk Structures:

Future approaches should consider obligation systems for artificial intelligence related occurrences. Deciding lawful structures for holding engineers, producers, and clients responsible in case of artificial intelligence framework disappointments, mishaps, or moral breaks is urgent for laying out a capable and just computer based intelligence environment.

9. **Constant Observing and Assessment:**

Dynamic Approach Systems:

Policymakers ought to take on unique approach structures that can develop close by innovative progressions. Constant observing and assessment of computer based intelligence applications and their cultural effect empower policymakers to make informed changes in accordance with guidelines. Adaptability in strategy structures considers iterative enhancements in light of true encounters.

Partner Commitment:

Strategies ought to order progressing partner commitment to guarantee that guidelines stay receptive to the necessities and worries of different partners. Normal discussions with industry delegates, promotion gatherings, analysts, and the overall population add to the advancement of approaches that are comprehensive, versatile, and intelligent of different points of view.

10. **Worldwide Emergency Reaction:**

Emergency courses of action for simulated intelligence Related Emergencies:

Policymakers ought to foster alternate courses of action for potential simulated intelligence related emergencies.

Expecting and getting ready for situations, for example, artificial intelligence driven network protection dangers, unseen side-effects, or framework disappointments is fundamental. Having powerful emergency reaction systems set up guarantees a quick and facilitated way to deal with relieve dangers and address unexpected difficulties.

Global Participation in Emergency Reaction:

Approaches ought to support worldwide participation in answering simulated intelligence related emergencies. Cooperative endeavors among countries and associations can work with the sharing of skill, assets, and best practices in emergency the executives. Policymakers ought to cultivate a culture of data trade and collaboration to address worldwide difficulties emerging from computer based intelligence innovations.

Chapter 7

AI in the Future: Trends and Predictions

The fate of Man-made consciousness (artificial intelligence) holds tremendous commitment and potential, forming the direction of innovative headways, cultural changes, and monetary scenes. As we peer into the distance of man-made intelligence, it becomes clear that few patterns and forecasts are ready to characterize the development of this extraordinary innovation. From headways in AI to the cultural effect of computer based intelligence applications, this investigation digs into the critical patterns and expectations that are probably going to describe the fate of man-made intelligence.

1. **Headways in AI:**
   Proceeded with Development of Profound Learning:
   AI, especially profound learning, is supposed to go through consistent advancement. Future progressions might prompt more modern brain network structures, empowering man-made intelligence frameworks to handle complex undertakings with

expanded proficiency and exactness.

The investigation of novel enactment capabilities, enhancement calculations, and model structures will add to the refinement of profound learning strategies.

Logical computer based intelligence (XAI):

As man-made intelligence frameworks become vital to dynamic in basic spaces, there is a developing accentuation on logic. Future patterns propose a coordinated exertion towards creating Logical simulated intelligence (XAI) strategies that give clear bits of knowledge into how man-made intelligence models come to explicit end results. This straightforwardness is critical for encouraging trust, responsibility, and moral utilization of computer based intelligence in applications like medical services, money, and law enforcement.

2. **Incorporation of computer based intelligence with Arising Innovations:**

Computer based intelligence and Quantum Processing:

The cooperative energy among computer based intelligence and quantum registering is ready to alter computational capacities. Quantum registering's capacity to deal with complex computations and cycle huge datasets in equal adjusts flawlessly with simulated intelligence's information concentrated nature. The combination of quantum figuring with computer based intelligence is supposed to open additional opportunities, speeding up artificial intelligence model preparation, advancement, and tackling issues that were beforehand computationally infeasible.

Artificial intelligence at the Edge:

Edge figuring, where information handling happens nearer to the wellspring of information as opposed to in unified cloud servers, is acquiring conspicuousness. Later on, computer based intelligence is expected to be progressively sent at the edge, empowering continuous dynamic in applications like independent vehicles, Web of Things (IoT) gadgets, and shrewd framework. This pattern lessens inactivity, improves protection, and monitors transfer speed.

3. **Simulated intelligence in Medical care:**

Customized Medication and Medication Disclosure:

Simulated intelligence's job in medical care is set to extend, especially in customized medication and medication disclosure. High level man-made intelligence calculations can investigate genomic information, distinguish designs, and foresee individual reactions to medicines. This customized approach holds the possibility to alter clinical medicines, upgrade drug disclosure cycles, and improve the viability of helpful intercessions.

Artificial intelligence Fueled Diagnostics:

The combination of artificial intelligence in analytic cycles is supposed to turn out to be more predominant. Simulated intelligence calculations, prepared on huge datasets of clinical pictures and patient records, can help medical care experts in more exact and ideal illness determination. From radiology to pathology, simulated intelligence controlled diagnostics can possibly work on early identification and treatment arranging.

4. **Independent Frameworks and Mechanical technology:**

Headways in Independent Vehicles:

The fate of transportation is firmly entwined with man-made intelligence, especially in the improvement of independent vehicles. Artificial intelligence driven frameworks are expected to assume a significant part in improving the security, productivity, and dependability of independent vehicles. Consistent upgrades in discernment, direction, and control calculations will make ready for broad reception of self-driving vehicles and other independent methods of transport.

Simulated intelligence in Mechanical technology:

Mechanical technology is set to observe critical progressions through the joining of computer based intelligence. Insightful robots equipped for gaining from their current circumstance, adjusting to dynamic situations, and teaming up with people are not too far off. From modern mechanization to medical services help, man-made intelligence fueled robots can possibly alter different areas, expanding human capacities and performing errands that are perilous or work escalated.

5. **Regular Language Handling (NLP) and Conversational computer based intelligence:**

Human-like Conversational Specialists:

Regular Language Handling (NLP) is supposed to progress, empowering the formation of additional human-like conversational specialists. Artificial intelligence models fit for figuring out setting, subtleties, and feelings in language will work with additional normal cooperations among people and machines. Conversational computer based intelligence applications, going from menial helpers to client assistance chatbots, will turn out to be progressively refined.

Multimodal man-made intelligence:

The fate of NLP will probably include the incorporation of multimodal abilities, empowering man-made intelligence frameworks to comprehend and produce content across different modalities, including text, pictures, and sound. This union of modalities will improve the extravagance and logic of artificial intelligence driven collaborations, taking into consideration more complete and instinctive correspondence.

6. **Artificial intelligence for Environmental Change and Manageability:**

Computer based intelligence for Natural Checking:

Computer based intelligence is ready to contribute essentially to tending to environmental change and advancing maintainability. High level simulated intelligence calculations can investigate huge scope ecological information, screen environment designs, and foresee catastrophic events. The utilization of simulated intelligence in ecological observing and protection endeavors is supposed to assume a significant part in relieving the effect of environmental change.

Energy Proficiency and Advancement:

In enterprises and shrewd framework, man-made intelligence applications zeroed in on energy productivity and streamlining are probably going to turn out to be more pervasive. Artificial intelligence driven frameworks can break down energy utilization designs, streamline asset allotment, and suggest maintainable practices. This pattern lines up with worldwide endeavors to decrease carbon impressions and advance naturally cognizant direction.

7. **Moral simulated intelligence and Mindful Development:**

Simulated intelligence Morals and Predisposition Alleviation:

The fate of artificial intelligence is inherently connected to moral contemplations and the moderation of predispositions. Policymakers, scientists, and industry pioneers are supposed to put a more grounded accentuation on creating computer based intelligence frameworks that stick to moral standards, stay away from oppressive results, and focus on reasonableness. Vigorous systems for reviewing and addressing predisposition in man-made intelligence calculations will be basic to mindful man-made intelligence development.

Mindful computer based intelligence Administration:

As computer based intelligence applications become more inescapable, there will be an increased spotlight on mindful computer based intelligence administration. Policymakers are probably going to create and refine administrative structures that advance responsibility, straightforwardness, and moral utilization of computer based intelligence innovations. Coordinated effort between state run administrations, industry, and common society will be fundamental in forming approaches that offset advancement with cultural prosperity.

8. **Simulated intelligence and Inventiveness:**
Generative simulated intelligence in Happy Creation:
Simulated intelligence's job in imaginative undertakings is ready to extend with the improvement of generative models. Man-made intelligence calculations fit for producing craftsmanship, music, writing, and different types of inventive substance will turn out to be more complex.

The cooperation between human makers and man-made intelligence apparatuses will lead to novel articulations of imagination, pushing the limits of what is conceivable in different creative spaces.

Simulated intelligence Upgraded Coordinated effort:
Joint effort among people and simulated intelligence is supposed to stretch out past satisfied creation. Artificial intelligence devices that increase human direction, critical thinking, and ideation cycles will become typical. Whether in business system, logical examination, or plan, simulated intelligence driven joint effort is expected to improve human abilities and cultivate imaginative answers for complex difficulties.

9. **Simulated intelligence in Training:**
Customized Opportunities for growth:
The fate of instruction is probably going to be molded by man-made intelligence driven customized growth opportunities. Versatile learning stages, controlled by simulated intelligence calculations, can fit instructive substance to individual understudy needs, learning styles, and progress. This customized approach can possibly advance instructive results and take care of assorted learning skills.

Man-made intelligence in Instructive Evaluation:
Man-made intelligence applications in instructive evaluation, for example, robotized reviewing frameworks and man-made intelligence driven coaching, are supposed to develop. These frameworks can give continuous input, distinguish regions where

understudies might require extra help, and add to additional viable and proficient instructive cycles. The reconciliation of man-made intelligence in training plans to upgrade openness and inclusivity in learning.

10. **Computer based intelligence and Network safety:**

Simulated intelligence Controlled Online protection Safeguard:
The fate of network protection will see expanded dependence on artificial intelligence fueled guard instruments. Computer based intelligence calculations can dissect huge datasets to recognize designs demonstrative of digital dangers, identify peculiarities, and answer security episodes progressively. The combination of computer based intelligence in online protection is significant for remaining in front of advancing digital dangers and guaranteeing the strength of computerized environments.

Antagonistic computer based intelligence and Online protection Difficulties:
As computer based intelligence is saddled for protective purposes, there is an equal concern with respect to ill-disposed computer based intelligence assaults. The future might observer the development of artificial intelligence driven digital dangers that influence modern procedures to dodge location. Policymakers and network protection specialists should consistently develop to address the advancing scene of antagonistic man-made intelligence and defend computerized foundations.

7.1 Advancements in AI Technology

The persevering walk of Man-made brainpower (simulated intelligence) innovation keeps on reshaping the scene of advancement, affecting ventures, society, and the manner in which we connect with the world. As we dive into the domain of progressions in computer based intelligence, a complex embroidery arises, woven with leap forwards in calculations, equipment, and applications. This investigation explores the multifaceted snare of late and expected progressions, revealing insight into the groundbreaking capability of artificial intelligence and its suggestions for what's in store.

1. **Development of AI Calculations:**
   Profound Learning Strength:
   The previous ten years has seen the ascendance of profound learning calculations, especially brain organizations, as the main impetus behind numerous computer based intelligence leap forwards. Profound learning's progressive and layered structure permits calculations to consequently gain complicated highlights from information, empowering phenomenal exactness in undertakings, for example, picture acknowledgment, normal language handling, and discourse amalgamation. The development of brain network designs, including convolutional brain organizations (CNNs) and repetitive brain organizations (RNNs), has pushed the abilities of man-made intelligence frameworks.
   Move Learning and Pre-prepared Models:
   Late headways have zeroed in on upgrading the proficiency of AI models through move learning and pre-prepared models. Move learning permits models prepared on one assignment to be reused for related undertakings, lessening the requirement for broad preparation datasets. Pre-prepared models, like OpenAI's GPT (Generative Pre-prepared Transformer) and BERT (Bidirectional Encoder Portrayals from Transformers), have exhibited astounding language grasping abilities, shaping the establishment for different normal language handling applications.

2. **Quantum Processing and simulated intelligence:**
   Quantum Matchless quality and simulated intelligence Applications:
   The crossing point of quantum figuring and computer based intelligence addresses an outskirts of investigation. Quantum processing's capacity to perform complex estimations in equal presents uncommon open doors for speeding up man-made

intelligence calculations. Quantum AI calculations, for example, quantum brain organizations and quantum support vector machines, hold the possibility to reform improvement assignments and take care of issues past the scope of traditional PCs. As quantum processors accomplish versatility and strength, their coordination with computer based intelligence is supposed to introduce another period of computational power.

Quantum AI Libraries:

Endeavors are in progress to foster quantum AI libraries that give a structure to executing quantum calculations in artificial intelligence applications. These libraries plan to work with the incorporation of quantum calculations into existing AI work processes, empowering scientists and specialists to outfit the force of quantum registering for advancement, recreation, and example acknowledgment undertakings.

3. **Support Learning Progressions:**
Profound Support Learning Leap forwards:
Support learning, a worldview where specialists figure out how to settle on choices through experimentation, has seen remarkable headways, especially in profound support learning. Calculations, for example, Profound Q-Organizations (DQN) and Proximal Approach Enhancement (PPO) have accomplished momentous accomplishments, including dominating complex games like Go and poker. The persistent refinement of support learning procedures adds to the advancement of man-made intelligence frameworks that show versatile and independent dynamic capacities.

Certifiable Applications:
Support learning is progressively tracking down applications in certifiable situations, going from mechanical technology to fund. In advanced mechanics, artificial intelligence frameworks influence support figuring out how to explore dynamic conditions, control protests, and improve control techniques. In finance, support learning calculations are utilized for portfolio enhancement,

algorithmic exchanging, and risk the executives, displaying the adaptability of this methodology in different spaces.

4. **Edge Figuring for computer based intelligence:**
Decentralized Handling:
The expansion of computer based intelligence at the edge denotes a change in outlook in registering engineering. Edge registering includes handling information nearer to the wellspring of age, lessening dormancy and data transfer capacity necessities. This is especially pivotal for applications like independent vehicles, Web of Things (IoT) gadgets, and constant picture acknowledgment, where low-inactivity reactions are basic. Man-made intelligence calculations sent at the edge empower gadgets to pursue independent choices without depending on unified cloud servers.

United Learning:
Combined learning is a vital progression in the domain of decentralized artificial intelligence. In unified learning, models are prepared across different decentralized gadgets or servers, safeguarding information protection and security. This cooperative learning approach is appropriate for applications where touchy information is involved, like medical services and money. Combined learning upgrades security as well as works with the advancement of strong and summed up models.

5. **Reasonable man-made intelligence (XAI):**
Interpretable Models:
As artificial intelligence frameworks become basic to dynamic in basic areas, the requirement for logic has acquired conspicuousness. Logical simulated intelligence (XAI) centers around creating models that give clear experiences into how they come to explicit end results. Interpretable AI models, for example, choice trees and direct models, are acquiring favor, particularly in applications where straightforwardness and responsibility are fundamental.

High level XAI Strategies:
Late headways in XAI incorporate methods that improve the

interpretability of perplexing models, like profound brain organizations. Techniques like layer-wise pertinence proliferation and consideration instruments add to understanding the inward activities of profound learning models. The improvement of cutting edge XAI methods expects to overcome any issues between the discovery idea of specific artificial intelligence models and the requirement for human-reasonable direction.

6. **Computer based intelligence for Inventiveness and Content Age:**

Generative Models:

The development of generative models has released a flood of imagination in man-made intelligence. Generative models, including Variational Autoencoders (VAEs) and Generative Antagonistic Organizations (GANs), have exhibited the capacity to make reasonable and novel substance across different spaces. From workmanship and music to composing and plan, computer based intelligence controlled generative models are extending the limits of human innovativeness.

Coordinated effort Among computer based intelligence and Craftsmen:

Artificial intelligence is progressively teaming up with craftsmen and makers to create cooperative works. Stages and apparatuses that influence generative man-made intelligence empower specialists to investigate new inventive conceivable outcomes, explore different avenues regarding styles, and stretch the boundaries of customary creative articulation. The harmonious connection among computer based intelligence and human innovativeness is encouraging another period of cooperative creativity.

7. **Computer based intelligence in Medical services and Biotechnology:**

Drug Revelation and Customized Medication:

Computer based intelligence is taking critical steps in altering medical care and biotechnology. In drug disclosure, man-made intelligence calculations dissect tremendous datasets to recognize potential medication applicants, foresee their viability, and upgrade sub-atomic designs. Customized medication, enabled by man-made intelligence, tailors medicines to individual hereditary profiles, working on restorative results and limiting unfriendly impacts.

Clinical Imaging and Conclusion:

The use of artificial intelligence in clinical imaging has reclassified symptomatic abilities. Computer based intelligence calculations break down clinical pictures, like X-beams and X-rays, with a degree of accuracy and speed that supplements human skill. Mechanized picture examination supports the early location of illnesses, improves indicative precision, and adds to more compelling treatment arranging.

8. **Normal Language Handling (NLP) Headways:**
   Context oriented Understanding:

   Progressions in Regular Language Handling (NLP) are directing towards logical comprehension. Cutting edge language models, as GPT-4, are intended to fathom setting, subtleties, and complicated phonetic designs.

   This logical comprehension empowers simulated intelligence applications to produce more sound and setting mindful reactions in conversational connection points and content creation.

   Multimodal NLP:

   The coordination of numerous modalities, like text, pictures, and sound, inside NLP systems is a blossoming pattern. Multimodal NLP permits simulated intelligence frameworks to comprehend and create content that consolidates data from different sources. This intermingling of modalities improves the expressive capacities of computer based intelligence applications, working with more thorough correspondence.

9. **Computer based intelligence and Advanced mechanics Coordinated effort:**

Human-Robot Cooperation:

Man-made intelligence is catalyzing headways in advanced mechanics, encouraging human-robot cooperation. Keen robots outfitted with man-made intelligence abilities are intended to work close by people, aiding errands that require aptitude, accuracy, and flexibility. From assembling and strategies to medical care and investigation, man-made intelligence fueled robots are enlarging human abilities and growing the extent of mechanical applications.

Computer based intelligence Morals in Mechanical technology:

The cooperation among artificial intelligence and mechanical technology has provoked conversations around moral contemplations. As robots outfitted with simulated intelligence become more coordinated into society, questions in regards to liability, responsibility, and moral use emerge. The advancement of moral systems for computer based intelligence driven mechanical technology is fundamental to explore the developing scene of human-robot cooperation.

7.2 Emerging Applications

The always growing scene of Man-made brainpower (computer based intelligence) keeps on divulging novel and extraordinary applications across assorted areas, reshaping enterprises and improving different parts of our regular routines. From medical services and money to training and diversion, the rise of simulated intelligence applications implies a change in perspective by they way we approach difficulties and influence innovation. This investigation digs into the thriving domain of arising applications, displaying the adaptability and effect of simulated intelligence in molding what's to come.

1. **Simulated intelligence in Environment Science and Ecological Observing:**

   Simulated intelligence is progressively turning into a strong partner in the battle against environmental change and the observing of ecological wellbeing. Environment researchers use man-made intelligence calculations to investigate immense datasets connected with weather conditions, sea flows, and barometrical circumstances. AI models can foresee outrageous climate occasions, survey the effect of environmental change, and add to the advancement of economical arrangements. In ecological observing, artificial intelligence is utilized to examine satellite symbolism, track deforestation, screen biodiversity, and distinguish regions in danger of catastrophic events, giving important bits of knowledge to protection endeavors.

2. **Artificial intelligence for Psychological well-being and Prosperity:**

The convergence of man-made intelligence and psychological wellness addresses a promising outskirts in medical care. Computer based intelligence applications are being created to aid the early identification of emotional wellness issues, customized treatment arranging, and ceaseless checking of people's prosperity. Chatbots and remote helpers furnished with regular language handling abilities offer help and take part in remedial discussions. Simulated intelligence driven feeling investigation and standard of conduct acknowledgment add to more nuanced evaluations, working with customized intercessions and decreasing the shame related with emotional well-being.

3. **Computer based intelligence in Medication Disclosure and Biomedical Exploration:**

The drug and biomedical exploration areas are encountering an unrest with the mix of computer based intelligence in drug disclosure and improvement. Man-made intelligence calculations dissect organic information, genomic data, and synthetic properties to distinguish potential medication competitors, anticipate their viability, and upgrade atomic designs. The speed increase of the medication disclosure process through simulated intelligence facilitates the advancement of new medicines as well as lessens expenses and upgrades the probability of progress in clinical preliminaries.

4. **Computer based intelligence Helped Innovativeness and Content Age:**

   Artificial intelligence is turning into a teammate in imaginative undertakings, extending its job past robotization and streamlining. Generative models, like GANs and VAEs, are utilized in different creative spaces, including visual expressions, music structure, and writing. Man-made intelligence produced content supplements human imagination, giving new points of view, styles, and conceivable outcomes. From making unique fine art to forming music and producing composing, computer based intelligence helped imagination is encouraging a powerful exchange among innovation and creative articulation.

5. **Computer based intelligence in Online protection and Danger Location:**

   The developing scene of digital dangers requests complex guard components, and computer based intelligence assumes an essential part in reinforcing online protection endeavors.

   Man-made intelligence fueled online protection frameworks utilize AI calculations to break down network traffic, recognize peculiarities, and distinguish designs characteristic of potential digital assaults. Social investigation, abnormality location, and prescient examination add to versatile danger discovery, permitting associations to answer proactively to arising digital dangers and strengthen their advanced safeguards.

6. **Simulated intelligence in HR and Ability The board:**

   HR (HR) divisions are tackling the abilities of computer based intelligence to smooth out ability the board cycles and improve labor force effectiveness. Man-made intelligence driven enrollment stages utilize normal language handling and AI calculations to dissect resumes, survey up-and-comer appropriateness, and anticipate work fit. Chatbots work with consistent correspondence during the enlistment cycle, while man-made intelligence based investigation give experiences into representative execution, commitment, and maintenance. The combination of simulated intelligence in HR adds to additional information driven navigation and a customized way to deal with ability the executives.

7. **Man-made intelligence in Agribusiness and Accuracy Cultivating:**

The rural area is embracing computer based intelligence to streamline cultivating practices and address the difficulties of food security. Artificial intelligence applications in agribusiness incorporate accuracy cultivating, where sensors, robots, and computer based intelligence calculations dissect information to enhance crop yields, screen soil wellbeing, and oversee water system. Prescient examination assist ranchers with expecting crop infections, improve asset portion, and upgrade generally speaking homestead efficiency. Simulated intelligence driven developments in horticulture add to maintainable practices, diminished ecological effect, and expanded productivity in food creation.

8. **Computer based intelligence in Expanded Reality (AR) and Augmented Reality (VR):**

The combination of man-made intelligence with AR and VR advances is opening vivid and intelligent encounters across different enterprises. In medical services, specialists use computer based intelligence improved AR to envision patient information during medical procedures, helping with accuracy and navigation. In schooling, artificial intelligence driven VR reenactments establish practical learning conditions for improved preparing. Man-made intelligence calculations dissect client conduct and inclinations to tailor vivid encounters, making a unique exchange between wise frameworks and virtual domains.

9. **Computer based intelligence in Independent Vehicles and Transportation:**

The time of independent vehicles is moved by man-made intelligence headways, changing the scene of transportation. Computer based intelligence calculations power self-driving vehicles, trucks, and robots, empowering them to explore complex conditions, decipher traffic conditions, and go with continuous choices.

Past independent driving, simulated intelligence adds to the improvement of transportation organizations, course arranging, and prescient support. The combination of simulated intelligence in transportation expects to improve security, lessen clog, and prepare for the fate of portability.

10. **Computer based intelligence in Space Investigation and Star-gazing:**

Computer based intelligence is stretching out its scope to the universe, helping with space investigation and cosmic exploration. AI calculations investigate huge datasets from telescopes and satellites, distinguishing divine items, ordering cosmic systems, and identifying exoplanets. Independent space apparatus influence artificial intelligence for route and dynamic during profound space missions. The marriage of artificial intelligence and space investigation speeds up logical revelations, advances mission arranging, and extends how we might interpret the universe.

7.3 Potential Societal Transformations

The approach of Man-made consciousness (computer based intelligence) is ready to introduce potential cultural changes that rise above mechanical development, reshaping the texture of our networks, economies, and lifestyles. As artificial intelligence proceeds to advance and penetrate different parts of society, the ramifications for social designs, administration, and human collaborations become progressively significant. This investigation dives into the potential cultural changes catalyzed by artificial intelligence, disentangling the valuable open doors and difficulties that lie not too far off.

1. **Monetary Outlook changes:**

Man-made intelligence's combination into businesses and working environments can possibly achieve critical monetary movements. Computerization, driven by simulated intelligence advancements, may reclassify the idea of work, prompting the uprooting of specific positions while setting out open doors for new, simulated intelligence driven jobs. The ascent of artificial intelligence fueled businesses could add to financial development, effectiveness, and advancement. Nonetheless, it likewise brings up issues about the dissemination of riches, professional stability, and the requirement for versatile instruction and labor force reskilling projects to line up with the requests of the developing position market.

2. **Reclassifying Work Elements:**
The effect of computer based intelligence on work elements reaches out past mechanization to the idea of coordinated effort among people and machines. While standard and dreary errands might be mechanized, there is a rising accentuation on human-machine cooperation in complex critical thinking, imagination, and direction. The cooperative energy among artificial intelligence and human knowledge could prompt the expansion of human capacities, encouraging a labor force that is versatile, inventive, and outfitted with cutting edge specialized abilities.

3. **Moral Contemplations in artificial intelligence Administration:**
The broad reception of computer based intelligence advances requires hearty moral systems and administration designs to address concerns connected with protection, inclination, straightforwardness, and responsibility. Cultural changes in administration will include the advancement of arrangements that guarantee mindful simulated intelligence sending, safeguard individual freedoms, and moderate the potential dangers related with artificial intelligence calculations. The moral contemplations in simulated intelligence administration stretch out to issues of decency, logic, and the evenhanded dissemination of the advantages of man-made intelligence across different populaces.

4. **Medical services Insurgency:**
Simulated intelligence's effect on medical care holds the commitment of extraordinary headways in diagnostics, customized medication, and patient consideration. Computer based intelligence calculations can break down clinical information with phenomenal speed and exactness, helping medical services experts in early illness location and therapy arranging. The expected cultural change in medical care includes a shift towards additional preventive and customized approaches, further developing well-being results and diminishing the weight on medical services frameworks.

5. **Instructive Worldview Advancements:**
As artificial intelligence turns out to be progressively coordinated into schooling systems, there is the potential for a change in perspective in how information is granted and procured. Versatile learning stages, controlled by simulated intelligence calculations, can fit instructive substance to individual understudy needs, learning styles, and progress. The center might move from customary state sanctioned testing to additional comprehensive evaluations that action decisive reasoning, critical thinking, and innovativeness. The democratization of instruction through internet based stages and artificial intelligence driven apparatuses could likewise improve openness and inclusivity.

6. **Rethinking Human-Machine Connections:**
The unavoidable presence of artificial intelligence in day to day existence might rethink human-machine connections, impacting the manner in which we cooperate with savvy frameworks. Conversational artificial intelligence, social robots, and menial helpers could become fundamental pieces of families and work environments, prompting more natural and customized client encounters. The potential cultural change lies in exploring the limits among human and man-made consciousness, cultivating joint effort, and addressing concerns connected with reliance,

protection, and the moral treatment of simulated intelligence elements.

7. **Upgraded Public Administrations:**
The coordination of simulated intelligence into public administrations can possibly improve proficiency, responsiveness, and inclusivity. Simulated intelligence driven arrangements in regions like transportation, metropolitan preparation, and public security can advance asset portion, further develop traffic the executives, and improve by and large city usefulness. Nonetheless, the change in broad daylight benefits additionally raises contemplations about information protection, security, and the evenhanded conveyance of man-made intelligence driven benefits across assorted networks.

8. **Social and Innovative Reshaping:**
Artificial intelligence's part in the imaginative space is developing, affecting creative articulation, content creation, and social creation. Generative man-made intelligence models can make craftsmanship, music, and writing, testing conventional ideas of imagination and initiation. The potential cultural change includes a unique interchange between human innovativeness and simulated intelligence help, prompting new types of social articulation and cooperative imaginative undertakings. The mix of man-made intelligence in the innovative approach might reclassify social standards and impact the development of imaginative disciplines.

9. **Security and Information Possession Difficulties:**
The unavoidable utilization of simulated intelligence depends on huge measures of information, raising worries about security, observation, and information proprietorship. The potential cultural change includes wrestling with the harmony between the advantages of man-made intelligence driven administrations and the assurance of individual protection. The development of guidelines, moral principles, and public mindfulness assumes an

essential part in molding a future where simulated intelligence coincides with a powerful structure for defending individual information.

10. Rethinking Social Communications:

The coordination of computer based intelligence into social stages, augmented reality, and specialized apparatuses can possibly rethink how people interface and associate. Artificial intelligence driven calculations may arrange content, customize suggestions, and impact the data people are presented to in their web-based connections. The potential cultural change lies in exploring the effect of simulated intelligence on friendly elements, data bubbles, and the general nature of human associations.

Chapter 8

The Road Ahead: Navigating the Future of AI

As we stand at the junction of mechanical advancement, the street ahead for Man-made consciousness (simulated intelligence) is cleared with both commitment and obligation. The direction of simulated intelligence's future is set apart by a powerful interchange of development, moral contemplations, and cultural effect. Exploring this way requires a comprehensive methodology that tends to the difficulties while outfitting the groundbreaking capability of man-made intelligence to improve humankind.

1. **Consistent Progressions in man-made intelligence Innovation:**

   The street ahead for computer based intelligence is inseparable from a constant quest for innovative progressions. Scientists and specialists are ready to push the limits of AI calculations, brain organizations, and computational capacities. The development of man-made intelligence innovation will observer forward leaps in reasonable man-made intelligence, quantum processing, and interdisciplinary joint efforts that meld computer based intelligence with other arising advancements. This ceaseless walk of development is a demonstration of the versatility and dynamism innate in the field of man-made intelligence.

2. **Moral and Capable computer based intelligence Improvement:**

As simulated intelligence turns out to be progressively implanted in the structure holding the system together, moral contemplations become the dominant focal point out and about ahead. Mindful computer based intelligence improvement involves resolving issues of predisposition, decency, straightforwardness, and responsibility. The moral arrangement of computer based intelligence includes the formation of hearty systems and rules that guarantee the innovation is lined up with human qualities, regards security, and maintains standards of value. The mix of moral contemplations into computer based intelligence advancement is vital for cultivating trust among clients and alleviating expected gambles.

3. **Coordinated effort Among People and simulated intelligence:**
The eventual fate of simulated intelligence imagines a cooperative scene where people and keen frameworks work synergistically. The street ahead includes planning computer based intelligence frameworks that expand human abilities, improving navigation, innovativeness, and critical thinking. Human-machine cooperation reaches out past mechanization, stressing an organization that use the qualities of the two substances. This cooperative worldview requires the improvement of man-made intelligence frameworks that are reasonable, interpretable, and fit for adjusting to human inclinations and values.

4. **Computer based intelligence for Social Great and Worldwide Difficulties:**
The street ahead for computer based intelligence is interlaced with a guarantee to utilizing the innovation for social great and

tending to worldwide difficulties. Computer based intelligence applications are being bridled to handle issues, for example, environmental change, medical care incongruities, and destitution. The improvement of computer based intelligence driven answers for philanthropic endeavors, debacle reaction, and practical advancement highlights the potential for innovation to be a power for positive cultural effect. The street forward includes adjusting man-made intelligence innovative work to the Unified Countries' Maintainable Improvement Objectives, making a guide for resolving squeezing worldwide issues.

5. **Comprehensive simulated intelligence Advancement and Access:**

   Guaranteeing that the advantages of man-made intelligence are open to everything is a critical part of the street ahead. Comprehensive man-made intelligence improvement includes effectively tending to predispositions in datasets, encouraging variety in the simulated intelligence labor force, and planning advancements that take care of a large number of clients. The democratization of man-made intelligence innovations expects endeavors to connect the computerized partition, giving evenhanded admittance to simulated intelligence apparatuses, training, and valuable open doors. The street ahead imagines a future where man-made intelligence adds to diminishing cultural imbalances instead of compounding them.

6. **Proceeded with Spotlight on Reasonableness and Interpretability:**

   The street ahead for simulated intelligence puts a proceeded with accentuation on the reasonableness and interpretability of simulated intelligence frameworks. As man-made intelligence calculations become more perplexing, understanding how they show up at choices becomes significant for client trust and moral organization. Analysts and engineers are effectively investigating strategies to make simulated intelligence frameworks more interpretable, permitting clients to fathom the thinking behind computer based intelligence driven results. This attention on reasonableness is crucial for applications in basic areas like medical care, money, and law enforcement.

7. **Tending to Predisposition and Decency Difficulties:**

The street ahead includes coordinated endeavors to address predisposition and reasonableness challenges in simulated intelligence frameworks. Predispositions present in preparing information can prompt unfair results, supporting cultural imbalances. Analysts and specialists are attempting to foster calculations and procedures that relieve predisposition, advance decency, and guarantee that man-made intelligence frameworks are even-handed across different segment gatherings. Handling predisposition in man-made intelligence requires a pledge to progressing assessment, straightforwardness, and responsibility in the turn of events and sending of shrewd frameworks.

8. **Moral Contemplations in man-made intelligence Administration:**

Administration systems for man-made intelligence are indispensable to exploring the street ahead. Moral contemplations in man-made intelligence administration include the foundation of clear approaches, guidelines, and norms that guide the dependable turn of events and sending of computer based intelligence advancements. Policymakers, industry pioneers, and specialists assume a cooperative part in forming administration structures that offset development with moral contemplations, defending against expected gambles, and guaranteeing that computer based intelligence benefits society at large.

9. **Public Mindfulness and Training:**

As man-made intelligence turns out to be progressively coordinated into day to day existence, public mindfulness and training assume a urgent part in exploring the street ahead. Building a very much educated society includes demystifying computer based intelligence, encouraging advanced proficiency, and engaging people to settle on educated conclusions about the utilization regarding computer based intelligence innovations. Instructive drives, public gatherings, and straightforward correspondence from simulated intelligence designers add to making a general public that is mindful of the capacities and ramifications of artificial intelligence.

10. **Proceeded with Exchange on simulated intelligence Morals:**

The street ahead requires a continuous and comprehensive exchange on man-made intelligence morals. Connecting with partners from assorted foundations, including ethicists, policymakers, technologists, and the overall population, is fundamental for molding the moral contemplations that guide computer based intelligence advancement. This discourse includes tending to complex moral issues, adjusting contending values, and guaranteeing that moral standards are implanted in the plan and sending of computer based intelligence frameworks. The street forward requires an aggregate obligation to moral simulated intelligence that reflects cultural qualities and desires.

8.1 Balancing Innovation and Regulation

The sensitive dance among development and guideline has for quite some time been a characterizing element of innovative advancement, and the domain of Man-made reasoning (simulated intelligence) is no special case. As artificial intelligence keeps on advancing, introducing phenomenal open doors and difficulties, tracking down the right balance between cultivating development and carrying out administrative measures becomes basic. Finding some kind of harmony is essential to saddling the extraordinary capability of simulated intelligence while addressing concerns connected with morals, security, and cultural effect.

1. **Cultivating Advancement:**
   At the core of the simulated intelligence scene is a steady drive for development. The dynamism of simulated intelligence innovative

work is filled by the journey for forward leaps in AI calculations, brain organizations, and applications that can alter enterprises. Cultivating development includes establishing a climate that energizes trial and error, coordinated effort, and chance taking. This involves offering help for research drives, encouraging inter-disciplinary methodologies, and boosting both public and confidential areas to put resources into artificial intelligence driven arrangements. A culture of development is critical for pushing the limits of what man-made intelligence can accomplish, from improving medical services to streamlining transportation frame-works.

2. **Moral Contemplations in Development:**

As advancement speeds up, moral contemplations should be joined into the texture of man-made intelligence improvement. The capable creation and sending of simulated intelligence inno-vations require a proactive way to deal with address concerns connected with inclination, decency, straightforwardness, and re-sponsibility. Moral rules give a compass to specialists, designers, and associations to explore the developing scene of simulated intelligence advancement. Coordinating morals into the develop-ment cycle guarantees that the advantages of man-made intelli-gence are saddled in a way that lines up with human qualities and cultural assumptions, moderating potential dangers related with unrestrained progression.

3. **Administrative Scene:**

The administrative scene for simulated intelligence is advancing, mirroring the need to lay out structures that oversee the capable utilization of this strong innovation. Administrative measures expect to guarantee that simulated intelligence applications stick to moral norms, shield individual protection, and limit likely cultural damages. States and global associations are effectively captivating in the advancement of administrative structures that balance the requirement for oversight with the basic to sustain development. The administrative scene is molded by continuous discoursed between policymakers, industry partners, and specialists, trying to make a powerful starting point for the moral organization of simulated intelligence.

4. **Security and Information Assurance:**
One of the focal worries in the guideline of simulated intelligence spins around security and information assurance. Simulated intelligence applications frequently depend on tremendous measures of information to prepare and work on their calculations. Finding some kind of harmony between using information for development and safeguarding individual security is a critical administrative test. Severe information security regulations and systems are being created to guarantee that client information is taken care of mindfully, with straightforwardness about how information is gathered, handled, and used. Adjusting the requirement for information driven advancement with security shields is crucial in building public trust and trust in simulated intelligence innovations.

5. **Predisposition and Decency Alleviation:**
Administrative endeavors are progressively centered around relieving predisposition and guaranteeing reasonableness in artificial intelligence frameworks. Predisposition in artificial intelligence calculations, frequently coming from one-sided preparing information, can prompt prejudicial results, supporting cultural imbalances. Guidelines plan to authorize measures that address predisposition in simulated intelligence models, advancing reasonableness, straightforwardness, and responsibility. Associations sending man-made intelligence are urged to direct customary reviews, appraisals, and effect examinations to distinguish and redress predisposition in their frameworks. The administrative scene expects to make a level battleground where simulated intelligence benefits are circulated evenhandedly across different segment gatherings.

6. **Responsibility and Straightforwardness:**

Guidelines encompassing simulated intelligence underscore the standards of responsibility and straightforwardness. Associations creating and conveying simulated intelligence frameworks are supposed to be straightforward about their strategies, dynamic cycles, and the ramifications of their advancements.

Laying out clear lines of responsibility guarantees that obligation regarding simulated intelligence results is suitably appointed. Straightforwardness measures, like reasonableness of artificial intelligence choices, enable clients and partners to comprehend and examine the working of artificial intelligence frameworks. These administrative parts add to building trust and trust in the dependable utilization of simulated intelligence.

7. **Worldwide Cooperation:**

The worldwide idea of simulated intelligence development requires global coordinated effort in molding administrative systems. Cross-line participation is fundamental for tending to difficulties that rise above public limits, for example, information sharing, interoperability, and normalization. Cooperative endeavors include sharing prescribed procedures, fitting administrative methodologies, and laying out normal moral rules that guide man-made intelligence improvement on a worldwide scale. Worldwide associations assume a critical part in encouraging this joint effort and guaranteeing a durable way to deal with the guideline of man-made intelligence innovations.

8. **Supporting a Powerful Environment:**

Administrative measures ought to be intended to sustain a powerful biological system where the two new businesses and laid out organizations can flourish. The nimbleness of new companies and little ventures is much of the time an impetus for problematic development in the simulated intelligence space. Administrative systems ought to try not to make hindrances that smother imagination and hinder the section of new players into the market.

Finding some kind of harmony includes fitting guidelines to various sizes of undertakings, empowering rivalry, and cultivating a climate where different voices and viewpoints add to the development of artificial intelligence.

9. **Expecting Potentially negative side-effects:**
The administrative scene ought to be dynamic and expectant, fit for tending to the potentially negative results of computer based intelligence development. As simulated intelligence innovations penetrate different spaces, there is a need to persistently assess and adjust administrative measures to stay up with developing difficulties. Proactive measures incorporate the foundation of administrative sandboxes, experimental runs programs, and progressing joint efforts between administrative bodies and the simulated intelligence local area. Expecting potentially negative results includes a criticism circle that empowers controllers to refine and refresh structures in light of genuine encounters and arising patterns.

10. **Public Commitment and Schooling:**

Administrative endeavors ought to be joined by vigorous public commitment and instruction drives. Illuminating the general population about the advantages and dangers of computer based intelligence innovations cultivates a more educated and participatory society.

Public information and criticism can be instrumental in molding administrative systems, guaranteeing that they reflect cultural qualities and assumptions. Schooling drives ought to engage people to grasp the ramifications of artificial intelligence in their regular routines, cultivating a feeling of organization and empowering them to settle on informed decisions.

8.2 Global Collaboration for Responsible AI

The turn of events and organization of Man-made reasoning (artificial intelligence) are worldwide undertakings that rise above lines and societies. As computer based intelligence innovations become progressively incorporated into different features of society, the basic for worldwide joint effort to guarantee mindful simulated intelligence rehearses turns out to be more evident. The intricacies and moral contemplations related with computer based intelligence require a purposeful exertion among countries, associations, and partners to encourage a cooperative methodology that shields moral standards, addresses difficulties, and guides the capable improvement of man-made intelligence on a worldwide scale.

1. **Shared Moral Standards:**
   Worldwide coordinated effort for capable man-made intelligence starts with the recognizable proof and understanding upon shared moral standards. The improvement of a generally acknowledged set of moral rules fills in as an establishment for dependable man-made intelligence rehearses. Standards like straightforwardness, decency, responsibility, and inclusivity give a typical system that can direct computer based intelligence improvement, guaranteeing that innovations are lined up with human qualities and regard for major privileges. Worldwide joint effort works with the harmonization of moral norms, taking into consideration a strong methodology that rises above individual countries' limits.

2. **Worldwide Associations as Facilitators:**
   Worldwide associations assume a critical part in working with worldwide cooperation for dependable simulated intelligence. Substances like the Unified Countries (UN), the Association for Monetary Co-activity and Advancement (OECD), and the World Financial Gathering (WEF) act as discussions where nations meet up to examine, intentional, and lay out rules for mindful artificial intelligence improvement. These associations give a stage to the trading of thoughts, best practices, and cooperative drives that add to forming the worldwide administration of computer based intelligence innovations.

3. **Normalization and Interoperability:**

   Fitting principles and guaranteeing interoperability are fundamental parts of worldwide joint effort in the artificial intelligence space. The variety of computer based intelligence innovations and applications requests a deliberate work to lay out normal principles that work with similarity and interoperability across borders.

   Worldwide bodies can work cooperatively to foster principles that address specialized angles, moral contemplations, and the interoperability of computer based intelligence frameworks. This normalization cultivates a strong worldwide environment where computer based intelligence innovations flawlessly incorporate and stick to normal standards.

4. **Cross-Line Exploration Joint efforts:**

   Headways in man-made intelligence frequently result from co-operative examination endeavors that rise above geological limits. Worldwide coordinated effort in simulated intelligence research includes pooling aptitude, assets, and information from scientists and organizations around the world. Cross-line coordinated efforts add to the variety of viewpoints, systems, and datasets, improving the advancement of man-made intelligence innovations. Cooperative exploration drives can address complex difficulties, improve the vigor of computer based intelligence models, and guarantee a more extensive comprehension of the moral ramifications related with man-made intelligence applications.

5. **Information Sharing and Security Conventions:**

   The capable utilization of computer based intelligence requires cautious thought of information sharing and protection conventions on a worldwide scale. Cross-line information streams are basic to the preparation and improvement of simulated intelligence models, yet they additionally raise concerns connected with security and information insurance. Global cooperation includes the foundation of conventions that balance the requirement for information driven advancement with the assurance of individual security freedoms. Settlements on information administration, secure information sharing instruments, and adherence to protection norms add to a worldwide climate where mindful computer based intelligence rehearses win.

6. **Tending to Inclination and Decency Universally:**

Simulated intelligence frameworks can unintentionally sustain predispositions present in preparing information, prompting out of line results. Worldwide cooperation is significant in tending to predisposition and guaranteeing decency in computer based intelligence applications. Shared drives can zero in on creating techniques for recognizing and relieving predisposition, advancing reasonableness in calculations, and laying out prescribed procedures that add to a more evenhanded organization of simulated intelligence advancements across different populaces. Cooperative endeavors assist with guaranteeing that simulated intelligence innovations are created with a worldwide viewpoint, representing the variety of clients and limiting prejudicial effects.

7. **Limit Building and Schooling:**

Worldwide cooperation reaches out to limit building and training drives that enable people and countries to capably explore the intricacies of artificial intelligence. Cooperative projects can work with information trade, preparing potential open doors, and the sharing of instructive assets.

These drives plan to fabricate a worldwide labor force furnished with the abilities to create, send, and oversee computer based intelligence innovations mindfully. Limit building endeavors cultivate a more comprehensive and fair support in the computer based intelligence scene, guaranteeing that different voices add to molding the eventual fate of simulated intelligence.

8. **Discretion for simulated intelligence Administration:**

As computer based intelligence turns into an international thought, conciliatory endeavors assume a critical part in encouraging worldwide joint effort for dependable simulated intelligence administration. Discretion includes the exchange of peaceful accords, deals, and shows that set up for moral simulated intelligence rehearses. Reciprocal and multilateral discoursed among countries add to the advancement of discretionary structures that advance dependable artificial intelligence improvement, relieve gambles, and lay out standards that guide the global local area in exploring the difficulties related with man-made intelligence advances.

9. **Emergency Reaction and Helpful Endeavors:**
Worldwide cooperation in artificial intelligence reaches out to emergency reaction and philanthropic endeavors. Computer based intelligence advances can possibly aid fiasco reaction, compassionate guide, and tending to worldwide difficulties like pandemics. Cooperative drives can zero in on creating computer based intelligence driven arrangements that upgrade the proficiency of emergency the board, further develop medical services results, and add to helpful endeavors all around the world. The mindful organization of simulated intelligence in emergency circumstances includes composed worldwide endeavors to guarantee the moral utilization of innovation for everyone's benefit.

10. **Comprehensive Administration Designs:**

Worldwide joint effort for dependable computer based intelligence requires the production of comprehensive administration structures that include portrayal from assorted partners. Comprehensive administration incorporates the support of legislatures, industry pioneers, common society, the scholarly world, and global associations. Stages for comprehensive exchange, for example, worldwide simulated intelligence culminations and gatherings, give potential open doors to partners to share viewpoints, add to policymaking, and aggregately shape the direction of man-made intelligence improvement. Comprehensive administration guarantees that choices with respect to man-made intelligence innovations mirror a wide range of interests and values.

8.3 Envisioning a Human-Centric AI Future

Imagining a future where Man-made consciousness (simulated intelligence) is intrinsically human-driven includes rising above the thought of man-made intelligence as a simple instrument or innovation and embracing a worldview where artificial intelligence frameworks are planned and sent to upgrade the human experience, cultivate inclusivity, and line up with human qualities. This vision requires a significant change by they way we consider, create, and coordinate man-made intelligence innovations into our social orders, setting the prosperity and strengthening of people at the very front of the computer based intelligence story.

1. **Expansion of Human Capacities:**

   A human-driven simulated intelligence future imagines simulated intelligence frameworks as partners that expand and intensify human capacities. As opposed to supplanting human undertakings, man-made intelligence advancements are intended to upgrade inventiveness, critical thinking, and navigation. This change in perspective underscores the cooperative connection among people and man-made intelligence, where keen frameworks go about as devices that enable people to accomplish more, cultivating an aggregate knowledge that joins the qualities of both.

2. **Comprehensive Plan and Openness:**

   In a human-driven computer based intelligence future, inclusivity is a core value in the plan and organization of computer based intelligence frameworks. Computer based intelligence innovations are made with a pledge to openness, guaranteeing that they are usable by people with different capacities, foundations, and requirements. Comprehensive plan includes thinking about a great many viewpoints, consolidating different datasets, and addressing possible predispositions to impartially make simulated intelligence frameworks that serve all citizenry.

3. **Enabling Personalization:**

Personalization turns into a foundation of a human-driven simulated intelligence future, where smart frameworks adjust to individual inclinations, requirements, and settings. Artificial intelligence advances are custom fitted to give customized encounters in training, medical care, amusement, and then some. This personalization stretches out past proposals to include versatile learning stages, medical services mediations in light of individual wellbeing profiles, and simulated intelligence driven devices that upgrade efficiency by understanding and adjusting to clients' novel working styles.

4. **Moral simulated intelligence Administration:**

A human-driven simulated intelligence future puts areas of strength for an on moral simulated intelligence administration, guaranteeing that artificial intelligence innovations stick to straightforward, responsible, and fair practices.

Moral rules oversee the whole lifecycle of computer based intelligence frameworks, from advancement to arrangement and then some. This includes vigorous components for recognizing and alleviating predispositions, straightforward dynamic cycles, and responsibility systems that consider associations and engineers answerable for the moral ramifications of their man-made intelligence advances.

5. **Straightforwardness and Logic:**

Straightforwardness and reasonableness are essential parts of a human-driven simulated intelligence future. Artificial intelligence frameworks are intended to give reasonable and interpretable experiences into their dynamic cycles. Clients are educated about how man-made intelligence calculations work, the information they depend on, and the reasoning behind their results. This straightforwardness cultivates trust and enables people to draw in with artificial intelligence advancements unhesitatingly, knowing how and why certain choices are made.

6. **Ceaseless Learning and Transformation:**
In a human-driven simulated intelligence future, simulated intelligence frameworks are dynamic and equipped for consistent learning and variation. As opposed to static apparatuses, these frameworks advance over the long run, gaining from client communications and criticism. This flexibility guarantees that computer based intelligence advances stay important, precise, and receptive to the developing necessities and inclinations of people and networks.

7. **Security by Plan:**
Security is a foremost worry in a human-driven computer based intelligence future, with computer based intelligence frameworks consolidating protection by-plan standards. These standards focus on the insurance of client information, limiting information assortment to what is fundamental, and executing powerful safety efforts. Clients have command over their own data, and associations stick to severe protection principles, establishing a believed climate where people have a real sense of safety in their connections with computer based intelligence advances.

8. **Artificial intelligence for Social Great:**
A human-driven computer based intelligence future imagines man-made intelligence innovations as useful assets for addressing cultural difficulties and adding to everyone's benefit. Simulated intelligence applications are bridled for medical services progressions, natural supportability, catastrophe reaction, and philanthropic endeavors. Cooperative drives influence simulated intelligence to handle worldwide issues, exhibiting the potential for insightful frameworks to be a power for positive social effect.

9. **Compassion and The ability to appreciate people on a profound level:**
The joining of sympathy and the capacity to understand

individuals on a deeper level into computer based intelligence frameworks is a critical part of a human-driven future.

Man-made intelligence advancements are intended to comprehend and answer human feelings, encouraging more normal and compassionate associations. This incorporates artificial intelligence driven remote helpers that perceive and adjust to clients' close to home states, as well as medical services applications that consider the profound prosperity of patients.

10. **Human Oversight and Control:**

Keeping up with human oversight and control is fundamental in a human-driven simulated intelligence future. While simulated intelligence frameworks contribute significant bits of knowledge and backing dynamic cycles, people hold extreme control. Computerized frameworks are planned with safeguards, and there are components for human mediation when essential. This approach guarantees that computer based intelligence innovations supplement human judgment, permitting people to settle on informed decisions directed by their qualities and inclinations.

Chapter 9

Conclusion

In the embroidery of mechanical development, the direction of Man-made reasoning (artificial intelligence) is a story that unfurls with significant ramifications for humankind. As we ponder the far reaching investigation of man-made intelligence — from its fundamental ideas to its mind boggling applications across different enterprises — the decision makes us to a pensive crossroads where the commitments and difficulties of this groundbreaking innovation merge.

At its center, the excursion through the sections of computer based intelligence discloses an account of development, versatility, and the steady quest for understanding and mirroring human knowledge. The definition and development of artificial intelligence typify the mechanical steps as well as the philosophical movements that shape our impression of what knowledge implies in a machine-driven world. The authentic outline mirrors the iterative idea of simulated intelligence improvement, featuring leap forwards, difficulties, and the advantageous connection between human inventiveness and AI calculations.

Key ideas and phrasing act as the structure blocks of a common language that pervades the multidisciplinary domain of man-made intelligence. As we explore the groundworks of artificial intelligence, it becomes clear that the phrasing portrays specialized perspectives as well as typifies the moral contemplations, cultural effect, and the complex interaction of calculations with living souls.

Digging into the domains of AI and profound learning disentangles the many-sided layers of man-made intelligence abilities. From regulated figuring out how to brain organizations, the profundity of AI procedures and the extraordinary force of profound learning designs highlight the flexibility and strength of man-made intelligence in tending to complex difficulties.

The investigation of brain organizations and calculations brings to the very front the many-sided instruments that support simulated intelligence independent direction. As we explore the scene of information, huge information, and simulated intelligence, the combination of these components reshapes enterprises, economies, and the actual texture of how data is handled and used in the cutting edge age.

The lacing of man-made intelligence with different ventures denotes a change in outlook in the manner in which we approach and lead business, medical care, money, fabricating, and then some. The parts devoted to every industry grandstand the extraordinary capability of man-made intelligence applications while highlighting the requirement for mindful administration, moral contemplations, and a human-driven approach.

The effect on medical services and medication is significant, with computer based intelligence arising as an impetus for diagnostics, therapy personalization, and medication revelation. The combination of man-made intelligence and money upsets conventional models, bringing about algorithmic exchanging, extortion discovery, and novel ways to deal with risk the executives. In assembling and computerization, computer based intelligence proclaims another time of effectiveness, accuracy, and flexibility, preparing for shrewd plants and advanced supply chains.

The horticultural area observes an extraordinary wave with accuracy cultivating and crop checking, exhibiting how man-made intelligence can add to reasonable practices and address worldwide food challenges. The parts committed to the working environment, work uprooting, and the basic for reskilling and upskilling dig into the many-sided elements of man-made intelligence and business, stressing the requirement for proactive techniques to explore the advancing position scene.

The moral contemplations woven all through the story resound as a clarion call for mindful man-made intelligence improvement. The investigation of inclination and decency, security concerns, and the basic for responsibility and straightforwardness highlights the complex moral difficulties that request nuanced arrangements.

In exploring these difficulties, man-made intelligence designers, policymakers, and society at large must team up to fashion moral systems that guide the dependable sending of computer based intelligence advances.

As we examine the cultural ramifications of artificial intelligence, the story grows past individual ventures to incorporate financial contemplations, training, admittance to computer based intelligence advances, and unofficial laws. The many-sided snare of worldwide cooperation, discretionary endeavors, and the plan of global norms arise as fundamental points of support for exploring the perplexing scene of artificial intelligence administration.

In imagining a future that is really human-driven, the end winds around together the yearnings for artificial intelligence expansion of human capacities, inclusivity in plan, moral administration, and the strengthening of people. The embroidery of a human-driven artificial intelligence future is one where innovation adjusts flawlessly with human qualities, improves personalization, and guarantees that sympathy and the capacity to understand individuals on a deeper level are indispensable parts of man-made intelligence communications.

As we stand at the intersection of mechanical advancement, the excursion through the sections of man-made intelligence uncovers the groundbreaking capability of wise frameworks as well as the significant obligation that goes with their turn of events and sending. The story welcomes us to embrace a future where advancement and guideline find some kind of harmony, where the cooperative endeavors of a worldwide local area make ready for mindful computer based intelligence practices, and where the moral contemplations directing artificial intelligence improvement mirror the common upsides of mankind.

In the ensemble of mechanical advancement, computer based intelligence arises as a strong harmony that reverberates across disciplines, businesses, and social orders. The finish of this investigation prompts contemplation, aggregate liability, and a guarantee to forming a computer based intelligence future that intensifies the human experience, encourages inclusivity, and lines up with the fundamental beliefs that characterize our common mankind. As we explore the strange regions of simulated intelligence's effect on businesses and society, the finishing up notes entice us to explore this groundbreaking excursion with shrewdness, moral stewardship, and an aggregate vision for a future where artificial intelligence fills in as a positive power to improve mankind.

9.1 Recap of Key Findings

As we navigate the diverse scene of "The Ascent of Man-made reasoning: Effect on Businesses and Society," an exhaustive summarization of key discoveries offers a blended comprehension of the unpredictable embroidery woven across the sections.

Every section dove into unmistakable features of simulated intelligence, unwinding its development, investigating its applications across enterprises, examining moral contemplations, and imagining a future where innovation amicably lines up with human qualities.

1. **Advancement and Definitions:**

   The excursion started with a basic investigation of the definition and development of simulated intelligence. From its beginning conceptualization to the contemporary time of AI and profound learning, simulated intelligence's direction arose as a powerful combination of logical interest, mechanical leap forwards, and the constant quest for imitating human insight.

2. **Authentic Outline:**

A review examination enlightened the verifiable achievements, exhibiting the back and forth movement of man-made intelligence improvement. From the good faith of the 1950s to the computer based intelligence winter and the resurgence in ongoing many years, the account highlighted the flexibility of the field and its responsiveness to mechanical, financial, and cultural changes.

3. **Key Ideas and Phrasing:**

Key ideas and phrasing filled in as the semantic platform for figuring out the complexities of computer based intelligence. From regulated figuring out how to brain organizations, the vocabulary of simulated intelligence typified specialized subtleties as well as moral contemplations, giving a common language to partners across different spaces.

4. **Underpinnings of simulated intelligence:**

Plunging further into the establishments, the investigation disclosed the perplexing structures that support man-made intelligence. The combination of information, calculations, and computational power arose as the bedrock, forming man-made intelligence's ability to dissect huge datasets, perceive designs, and create experiences that rethink dynamic cycles across businesses.

5. **AI and Profound Learning:**

AI and profound learning arose as the powerful motors impelling man-made intelligence's extraordinary potential. Directed and unaided learning, supported by the profundity of brain organizations, exhibited the flexibility and viability of artificial intelligence calculations, denoting a change in outlook in how machines learn and develop.

6. **Brain Organizations and Calculations:**
The account then, at that point, dug into the intricate landscape of brain organizations and calculations, uncovering the modern components that work with artificial intelligence independent direction.

From convolutional brain networks in picture acknowledgment to repetitive brain networks in grouping handling, the sections enlightened the flexibility of man-made intelligence models.

7. **Information, Enormous Information, and simulated intelligence:**
The marriage of man-made intelligence with information, particularly large information, arose as a urgent section. The collaboration among computer based intelligence and sweeping datasets filled headways, changing how associations gather experiences, make expectations, and advance activities in the time of data overflow.

8. **Simulated intelligence in Ventures: An Exhaustive Outline:**
The account spread into explicit ventures, uncovering how computer based intelligence's extraordinary touch reshapes areas like medical services, money, assembling, and farming. From accuracy cultivating to algorithmic exchanging, simulated intelligence's engraving on assorted areas represented its ability to change processes, upgrade productivity, and drive development.

9. **Medical care and Medication:**
The effect on medical care and medication arose as a piercing part, portraying man-made intelligence's job in diagnostics, therapy personalization, and medication revelation. The convergence of innovation and medical services guaranteed better understanding results, smoothed out processes, and the possibility to address longstanding difficulties in the clinical field.

10. **Working environment, Business, and Upskilling:**
The developing elements of the work environment in the period of computer based intelligence blended reflections on work

removal, reskilling goals, and the perplexing exchange among human and machine. The story unfurled as a call for proactive procedures, stressing the significance of setting up the labor force for the developing requests of the gig market.

11. **Moral Contemplations:**
Moral contemplations arose as an intermittent theme, highlighting the basic for dependable man-made intelligence improvement. The parts fastidiously investigated predispositions and decency, security concerns, and the significant requirement for straightforwardness and responsibility in artificial intelligence frameworks, outlining moral situations that request nuanced arrangements.

12. **Worldwide Joint effort for Mindful man-made intelligence:**
Worldwide joint effort arose as a core value for guiding the moral direction of man-made intelligence. From shared moral standards to global associations working with exchange, the story unfurled as a demonstration of the need of cooperative endeavors in forming capable artificial intelligence administration.

13. **Imagining a Human-Driven simulated intelligence Future:**

The finishing up sections imagined a future where computer based intelligence isn't simply a device however a compassionate colleague, enlarging human capacities while focusing on inclusivity, straightforwardness, and personalization. The human-driven story prepared for an amicable mix of man-made intelligence into the structure holding the system together, lining up with our qualities and engaging people.

Basically, the restatement of key discoveries combines into an extensive mosaic that catches the embodiment of man-made intelligence's excursion — from its calculated beginning to its significant effect on ventures and society. Every section adds a layer of understanding to the multifaceted story, offering experiences, bringing up issues, and provoking an aggregate thought on the mindful and moral direction of artificial intelligence as it keeps on rising in the mechanical scene.

9.2 Call to Action for Stakeholders

As the story of "The Ascent of Man-made reasoning: Effect on Businesses and Society" unfurls, a convincing source of inspiration resounds, gathering partners from different domains — be they policymakers, industry pioneers, specialists, or the overall population — to connect effectively in molding the direction of artificial intelligence. The groundbreaking force of simulated intelligence is certain, however with this power comes the obligation to explore its effect morally, comprehensively, and with an aggregate obligation to the prosperity of humankind.

1. **Policymakers and Controllers:**
   At the front of the source of inspiration stand policymakers and controllers entrusted with creating the structures that administer man-made intelligence improvement and sending. The powerful idea of computer based intelligence requires proactive, versatile arrangements that offset development with moral contemplations. Policymakers ought to team up across boundaries to lay out worldwide norms, cultivating a durable worldwide way to deal with simulated intelligence administration. These systems should focus on straightforwardness, responsibility, and the assurance of individual privileges, moderating the potential dangers related with uncontrolled computer based intelligence progression. Policymakers hold the way to molding a climate where man-made intelligence development adjusts consistently with cultural qualities and assumptions.

2. **Industry Pioneers and Trailblazers:**
   Industry pioneers and trailblazers assume a significant part in guiding the course of man-made intelligence's effect. The source of inspiration beseeches them to focus on capable man-made intelligence works on, installing moral contemplations into the DNA of their associations.

   From algorithmic straightforwardness to tending to predisposition in computer based intelligence frameworks, industry pioneers should show others how its done, exhibiting a promise to decency, inclusivity, and responsibility. Coordinated effort with policymakers, analysts, and promotion bunches is fundamental to explore the moral components of artificial intelligence by and large. Industry pioneers are not simply spearheads; they are stewards of an innovation that significantly impacts the world, and their activities resonate across society.

3. **Specialists and The scholarly world:**

The source of inspiration reaches out to scientists and the scholarly community, the draftsmen of simulated intelligence's establishments. The basic is to lead research with a moral compass, focusing on decency, straightforwardness, and the aversion of predisposition. Cooperation across disciplines and organizations cultivates a comprehensive comprehension of the cultural ramifications of computer based intelligence, directing the improvement of dependable innovations. Analysts should effectively add to the continuous talk on computer based intelligence morals, sharing experiences, best practices, and examples learned. The moral contemplations of simulated intelligence are as essential to investigate as the actual calculations, and specialists hold the obligation to shape a future where computer based intelligence adjusts consistently with human qualities.

4. **Organizations and Companies:**

Organizations and companies employ significant impact in the reception and sending of simulated intelligence advances. The source of inspiration begs them to coordinate dependable simulated intelligence rehearses into their procedures. This includes straightforwardness in simulated intelligence dynamic cycles, guaranteeing fair and impartial calculations, and focusing on client security. Organizations ought to put resources into computer based intelligence schooling and preparing for their labor force, recognizing the developing idea of work in the computer based intelligence period. By cultivating a culture of mindful man-made intelligence inside their associations, organizations add to building entrust with customers and society at large.

5. **The Labor force:**

A proactive source of inspiration resounds for the labor force, encouraging people to embrace an outlook of persistent learning and transformation. As man-made intelligence changes enterprises and occupation scenes, the basic is to participate in up-skilling and reskilling drives. The labor force representing things to come should be deft, furnished with the abilities that supplement artificial intelligence innovations instead of go up against them. People ought to effectively look for open doors for learning and advancement, perceiving the cooperative connection between human aptitude and computer based intelligence abilities. Enabling the labor force guarantees that the advantages of simulated intelligence are appropriated comprehensively, limiting the gamble of occupation relocation.

6. **Support Gatherings and Common Society:**

Support gatherings and common society assume a pivotal part in considering partners responsible. The source of inspiration encourages these gatherings to enhance their voices in molding computer based intelligence strategies, pushing for straightforwardness, responsibility, and moral contemplations. By encouraging public mindfulness and commitment, promotion bunches add to a more educated and participatory society. They act as guard dogs, guaranteeing that the arrangement of computer based intelligence advancements lines up with majority rule values, common liberties, and the more extensive interests of the local area.

7. **Instructive Establishments:**

Instructive establishments bear the obligation of setting up the cutting edge for an existence where man-made intelligence is pervasive. The source of inspiration for instructors is to incorporate artificial intelligence education into educational plans, cultivating a comprehension of the innovation's standards, applications, and moral ramifications. Understudies ought to be furnished with decisive reasoning abilities that engage them to explore the mind boggling scene of simulated intelligence. Instructive foundations act as the hatcheries for moral computer based intelligence designers, policymakers, and specialists, molding a future where the combination of artificial intelligence adjusts flawlessly with cultural qualities.

8. **Worldwide Joint effort:**

A resonating source of inspiration is coordinated towards cultivating worldwide cooperation. The difficulties and amazing open doors introduced by computer based intelligence rise above borders, requesting global participation. Policymakers, industry pioneers, scientists, and promotion gatherings ought to effectively take part in worldwide discussions, cooperative drives, and discoursed that shape the moral administration of simulated intelligence. By sharing prescribed procedures, orchestrating principles, and on the whole tending to the moral components of simulated intelligence, a worldwide local area can explore the intricacies of this groundbreaking innovation.

9. **Public Commitment:**

The last harmony in the source of inspiration is coordinated towards the overall population. Educated and connected with residents are fundamental for guiding the moral direction of artificial intelligence. General society ought to effectively take part in conversations, remain informed about computer based intelligence advancements, and voice their interests and assumptions. By cultivating a culture of capable computer based intelligence use and considering partners responsible, people in general turns into a main impetus in molding a computer based intelligence future that lines up with cultural qualities.

9 788196 837440